NEW FRONTIERS IN EDUCATION

NEW FRONTIERS IN EDUCATION

Mohit Chakrabarti

KANISHKA PUBLISHERS, DISTRIBUTORS
NEW DELHI-110 002

KANISHKA PUBLISHERS, DISTRIBUTORS
4697/5-21 A, Ansari Road, Daryaganj
New Delhi-110 002
Phones : 2327 0497, 2328 8285
Fax : 011-2328 8285
E-mail: kanishka_publishing@yahoo.co.in

First Published 2008

ISBN 978-81-8457-034-2

PRINTED IN INDIA

Published by Madan Sachdeva for Kanishka Publishers, Distributors, 4697/5-21A, Ansari Road, Daryaganj, New Delhi-110 002, Typeset by Sunshine Graphics, Delhi, and Printed at Nice Printing Press, Delhi.

DEDICATED TO

Professor Debnarayan Chattopadhyay, Burdwan Raj College, University of Burdwan
and
Professor Prodyot Kumar Maity
Burdwan Raj College, University of Burdwan

Preface

Education is now-a-days at the crossroads of advancement and predicaments. While education of the child is yet to negotiate the essentials of appropriate advancement in learning and teaching, it also suffers from devaluation of values especially directed towards natural and spontaneous efflorescence of creativity and aesthetic consciousness. "Child Education: Priorities and Promises" probes into these ends-in-view and suggests a few arresting breakthroughs.

Motivation in education plays a very significant role in meaningful and worthwhile education. Indeed, setting newer and more refreshing agenda of motivation in communication education in tune with teaching-learning acts as a living and positive force in all round development. "Communication Education: Setting New Agenda of Motivation" is an earnest endeavour at unfolding a few yet-to-be considered perspectives of education.

"Accelerating Quality Improvement in Community Mobilisation: Aesthetic Parameters" and "Education for Probing into the Learners' World: Aesthetic Dimensions" might attract the attention of revered readers.

With education as one of the human rights as guaranteed in the constitution, the promises and priority areas necessitate a re-thinking in response to the wishes and aspirations of a rapidly changing Indian society. The dynamics of advancement in education awaits more dedication and greater involvements in newer frontiers. "Education and Constitutional Provisions in Human Rights" is a critical study in this regard.

"Exploring Quality in Child Education: Aesthetic Avenues" is an in-depth study on the role of aesthetics in child education for quality crystallisation and might evoke thrilling stylistics in quality enhancement.

"Education of the Future: Sri Aurobindo's Vision" may be considered a definite and profound pointer to enlightened advancement of education in the new millennium.

That true education is always inclusive and cordially conjoint in an ambience of altruistic and communicative experiences has been critically analysed in "Inclusive Education: Prioritising Vibrant Vision", which might call forth worthy dividends from esteemed readers.

"Living Education: Vivekananda's Viewpoints" and "Relevance of Tagore's Creative Thinking in the New Millennium" might set forth new frontiers of education in perfect symphony with the vibrant and illumined thoughts of Swami Vivekananda and Rabindranath Tagore, the two masterminds in education as it ought to be right now and for centuries to come.

Sobdo Chakrabarti, my son, has taken all care in the computer processing of the work. Best wishes, Sobdo!

If the book contributes a little to the world of education and enjoys endearing warmth of acceptance from every esteemed reader, I would murmur in serenity within myself the most inspiring words of Tagore: "In the meanwhile the air is filling with the perfume of promise."

Seemantika **Mohit Chakrabarti**

Seemanto Palli
Santiniketan-731 235
INDIA

Contents

1

CHILD EDUCATION: PRIORITIES AND PROMISES

Education is a challenging task. Child education is perhaps more challenging because it calls forth more devotion and dedication than in any other spheres of education. It also demands a certain positive mental attitude towards hapless children who are, for reasons beyond their power and control, terribly neglected and more or less socially ill-treated, thanks to rapid industrialisation and urbanisation in a care-free spree of a rampantly robotised modern society. That education of and for the child is even now at the back seat can be easily proved from a study of child labour and allied ukase leading to absence of appropriate education at the very crucial stage of human life.

The recent scenario of negotiating pitfalls in child education is all but satisfactory. Lopsided planning, reality-shy programmes of action, involvement of inefficient teaching personnel and, above all, absence of persuasive plus dynamic administrative operation—all these have affected the education of the child so much so that the number of stop-outs and stagnation is gradually becoming increasingly alarming and ominous. In addition, the war-foot strategies for eradication of illiteracy in diverse forms like operation blackboard, mid-day meal programmes and so on had earned very poor response for reasons best known to anyone who cares and probes into the very entrails of work schedules. As a matter of fact, it has recently been studied that the government in its common minimum programme has failed to fulfil the pledge of spending 6 per cent of the national income on education. With unusually low government spending for education dropping from 10.9 per cent of the total outlay (1995-96) to 9.23 (2004-05) perhaps the worst sector is the education of the child. The recent significant analytical and evaluative study by the Aga Khan Education Foundation on the universalisation of primary education under the programme of Sarva Shiksha Abhiyan is noteworthy: "The study brings out the gap between the required magnitude of additional financial resources for universalisation of elementary education and the actual additional spending from 1998-99 to 2005-06 at the national level."

Admittedly, the colossal task of addressing the constraints in the uninterrupted education of every child throughout the country should not be rest assured with mere identification but should definitely call forth greater involvement especially in the financial sector. As the Foundation characteristically observes, "The major factors affecting the resource-absorption capacity of states have been traced to bottlenecks in the planning and budgetary processes that are being followed under Sarva Shiksha Abhiyan." A systematic, disciplined and regular flow of funds contributing to a healthy climate of teaching-learning in the sphere of child education in every nook and corner of the country and its apposite utilisation are yet far below expectation.

Meanwhile, motivation spurt in child education is hopelessly low. How to motivate the child in learning is a key factor in consolidation and advancement in education. The essential strategies for better motivation like identification, mapping, selecting, analysing, executing and evaluating are vital to strengthening the programmes of teaching for which the teacher must be proactive and painstaking, diligent and persevering. Interesting programmes for quality in child education can very well be directed towards inspiring the child to learn how to solve all its intrinsic irrelevances and inconsistencies and restructure existing ideas and concepts as and when necessary. In this connection, the motivation programme in order to facilitate the child how to learn by reacting to counter-intuitive information as chalked out by Vosniadou is:

(a) Teachers need to be aware that students have prior beliefs and incomplete understandings that can conflict with what is being taught in school.
(b) It is important to create the circumstances where alternative beliefs and explanations can be externalized and expressed.
(c) Teachers need to build on the existing ideas of students and slowly lead them to more mature understandings. Ignoring prior beliefs can lead to the formation of misconceptions.
(d) Students must be provided with observations and experiments that have the potential of showing to them that some of their beliefs can be wrong. Examples from the history of science can be used for this purpose.
(e) Scientific explanations must be presented with clarity and, when possible, exemplified with models.
(f) Students must be given enough time to restructure their prior conceptions. In order to do this, it is better to design curricula that deal with fewer topics in greater depth than attempting to cover a great deal of topics in a superficial manner.[1]

Undeniably, restructuring, redesigning and reassuring a vibrant curriculum is crucial to the creation of a child-caring learning climate in education. At present, textbooks, for example, for children are dull and devoid of stimulant reading matters in many subjects. Children hardly come across living books written in compliance with their world of out-of-the-track ideas and innovative promises of perfection. Besides these, stereotyped dealings with children's channels of thought-patterns particularly in a heterogeneous classroom climate miserably fail to ignite their enviable illuminating visions. This is all the more explicit in the exercise and development of their creative and critical thinking where mechanical learning is continually dumping all rubbish in the name of purposeful and meaningful learning. In fact, teaching children with warm love and affection for an endearing and natural pace of progress is rapidly deteriorating, thanks to free encroachment of electronic gadgets readily available for moratorium of child creativity. Today's children are more presented with sensitivity paranoia than with undisturbed world of freedom.

Shockingly, the education of sympathy for children has been shown the door. Instead, apathy and ignorance have taken the driver's seat in the rat race of child education. We are yet to pay heed to the invaluable fact so categorically expressed by Rabindranath Tagore: "Apathy and ignorance are the worst forms of bondage for man." Anyone who wants to have a glimpse of the lost world of children in spontaneous and self-enriching education would be simply surprised to know from a recent report that nearly 17.04 per cent of children suffer from abuses which are hardly disclosed. Broken families, unhygienic conditions for physical and mental development and forced labour still await stringent measures for eradication and rehabilitation of support system. The curriculum for child education also deserves reframing and reorienting from psycho-social and cultural parameters.

Knowledge explosion and culture, too, look forward newer ambience of understanding and experimentation. A harmonious blending of children's knowledge and the knowledge of the locality would certainly contribute to consolidation of what the child knows and feels, reacts and probes. As the National Curriculum Framework 2005 characteristically observes:

> Day-after-day children bring to school their experiences of the world around them the trees that they have climbed, the fruits they have eaten, the birds they have admired. All children are alive to the natural cycles of day and night, of the weather, the water, the plants and the animals that surround them. Children, when they enter Class I, already have a rich language base of small numbers, and the rudiments of operations are already in place. Yet rarely do we hear the

knowledge that they already have and which they bring into the classroom. Rarely do we ask children to talk about or refer to the world outside the school during our lessons and teaching. Instead we resort to the convenience of the printed word and picture, all of which are poor replicas of the natural world. Worse still, today in the name of computer-aided learning, the living world is being turned into animation strips that children are expected to watch on their computer screens. Before starting a lesson on living and non-living, if a teacher was to take her class out on a walk through a field near the school, and on returning asked each child to write the names of ten living things and ten non-living things that she/he saw, the results would be amazing. Children in Mahabalipuram in Tamil Nadu may include in their list of things sea shells, pebbles and fish, and those in Chhattisgarh near the Dandakaranya forest may include nest, bee hive, and anklet. Instead, children are usually required to look at a drawing in the textbook, or a list of words, and sort the things out as living and non-living.[2]

Apathy to and ignorance of natural learning resource for sustainable and healthy generation of knowledge in child education are at the grassroots of crisis in quality education. Information schedules for the learner child necessitate a complete and radical overhauling with freedom and love as the parameters of progress. The world of imagination and fantasy so fascinating and stimulating to the child in the pursuit of knowledge should be revived and rejuvenated with a mindset alive and afresh with the spirit of adventure. Life thus fondled and caressed with sufficient platforms of interaction with precious little learners who know best what to select and how to select in the process of learning.

The world of joy in the mind of the child learner, too, is hopelessly imprisoned in dumb silence. The regular and routine-oriented heavy course of studies right from the flaming years of joy has utterly plundered the pompous possibilities of learning in and through exciting experiences well-encountered by the behavioural manifestation of every child. Consequently, many children suffer from fear psychosis where joy in her/his traits of personality is, as it were, considered an unwanted guest. What an irony in the name of education!

Apart from the fact that the child receives an extra impetus from the joy of learning, the highest dividend in education is assuredly received from beauty. Unfortunately, the aesthetic education of beauty is almost alien to the child in the present day system of education where individualised and ardent instruction on child creativity and sincere handling of the appreciation faculties of children are yet to be properly addressed. Undeniably, a little bit of sharing, enjoying and appreciating the very nuances of beauty as spontaneously reflected in terms of child imagination would certainly contribute a lot to learning the treasure within.

As regards the role of quality acceleration in teacher education for advancement of child education in the right direction the task ahead is legion. It is absolutely true that unless quality teachers are available in child education, no fruitful purpose in dealing with the stop outs and stagnancies so alarmingly aggravating would be served. It is time to address the following:

(i) Introducing package programmes of training programmes in-service and pre-service primary teacher education.

(ii) Holding seminars, conferences, symposia, workshops etc., on contents and methods of teaching different school subjects.

(iii) Exercising innovative programmes of activities on preparation of interesting and thought provoking textbooks for children.

(iv) Occasional excursions, study tours, nature studies, etc., in order to consolidate and fillip children's own constructive and critical imaginative and aesthetic patterns and peculiarities of observations.

(*v*) Studies and researches on recent trends and tendencies in child education.

A well-planned transfer from textbooks mainly written for multi-grade organised group classroom students to mono-grade ones with a view to ensuring better efflorescence of child education is the need of the hour. Indeed, introducing different types of teaching strategies for different learners leads to perfection in teaching-learning. As it is rightly suggested:

(*i*) Thematic lesson with a variety of exercises and activities at different levels for different groups.
(*ii*) Graded self-access materials that children can engage with on their own with minimum scaffolding from the teacher, allowing them to work on their own or with other children.
(*iii*) Whole-group activity plans, say, story-telling or performing a small drama, based on which children can do different activities. For example, all children from classes I to V may enact the folk story of the rabbit and the lion together, and after this groups I and II may work with flashcards with the names of various animals; groups III and IV may make a series of drawings and then write out the story against each drawing, working in small groups; and group V may write the story, suggesting alternative endings to it. Without the support of appropriate materials, most teachers find themselves trying to juggle mono-grade class groups, with the result that for the majority of children, time on the task becomes very low.[3]

Appeal to the child's innate and innovative qualities is the key to success in teaching. A sincere teacher gives priorities to this very fact and allows the child to march ahead by self-efflorescence and self-activity in an ideal atmosphere of freedom and joy in learning. In the invaluable words of Sri Aurobindo:

> Every child is a lover of interesting narrative, a hero-worshipper and a patriot. Appeal to these qualities in

him through them let him master without knowing it the living and human parts of his nation's history. Every child is an inquirer, an investigator, analyser, a merciless anatomist. Appeal to those qualities in him and let him acquire without knowing it the right temper and the necessary fundamental knowledge of the scientist. Every child has an insatiable intellectual curiosity and turn for metaphysical enquiry. Use it to draw him on slowly to an understanding of the world and himself. Every child has the gift of imitation and a touch of imaginative power. Use it to give him the groundwork of the faculty of the artist.

It is by allowing Nature to work that we get the benefit of the gifts that she has bestowed to us. Humanity in its education of children has chosen to thwart and hamper her processes and, by so doing, has done much to thwart and hamper the rapidity of its onward march. Happily, saner ideas are now beginning to prevail. But the way has not yet been found. The past hangs about our necks with all its prejudices and errors and will not leave us; it enters into our most radical attempts to return to the guidance of the all-wise Mother. We must have the courage to take up clearer knowledge and apply it fearlessly in the interest of posterity. Teaching by snippets must be relegated to the lumber-room of dead sorrows. The first work is to interest the child in life, work and knowledge, to develop his instruments of knowledge with the utmost thoroughness, to give him mastery of the medium he must use. Afterwards, the rapidity with which he will learn will make up for any delay in taking up regular studies, and it will be found that, where now he learns a few things badly, then he will learn many things thoroughly well.[4]

The growing child must be taught by the teacher with a loving and affectionate touch. The young learner should definitely be identified all the time by the latter with the youthful vitality of his own mind. This will create a sense of oneness, togetherness and conjoint adventure into the world of education with all assurances of kinship between the learner and the teacher. Therefore, knowing children as young ones and not like adults and being familiar and identified with their behaviour-patterns are the essentials for quality teaching. What should be the strategies to be adopted by the teacher in this regard? Here is an answer worth emulating and significant:

> They [Children] are quite unlike adults. They are so different that it would be easier to understand them if they looked like animals. You know how a baby, before it is born, passes through the main stages of evolution. It begins by looking like an amoeba, goes on to look like a fish, resembles a big-headed monkey for some time, and ends up at birth still looking remarkably like a little red blind clutching grimacing ape. I have often thought that in its first fifteen years of life it passes through another series of animal existences. Boys of nine and ten, for instance, are very like dogs. Watch a pack of them hot on the scent, yapping, running and jumping, bouncing aimlessly around full of energy, kicking one another or breaking down a door as carelessly as a dog nips at its neighbour's flanks or bursts through a hedge. When they are really enjoying the chase, all their teeth and eyes gleam and their breath and laughter go "huh, huh, huh, huh" like a leash of fox-terriers. Girls in their middle teens are like horses, strong, nervous, given to sudden illnesses and inexplicable terrors, able to work remarkably hard if they are kept firmly in hand, but really happiest when they are thinking of nothing in particular and prancing about with their manes flying. Both dogs and horses are amiable creatures and can be domesticated, but it is a mistake to treat them as though they were human. It is also a mistake to treat horses as though they were dogs, or dogs like horses.

So, if you are interested in teaching, do not even expect the young to be like yourself and the people you know. Learn the peculiar patterns of their thought and emotions just as you would learn to understand horses or dogs—or other animals (for there are all kinds of different animals implicit in children: the very small ones are often more like birds)—and then you will find that many of the inexplicable things they do are easy to understand, many of the unpardonable things easy to forget.

How can you learn this? Chiefly by experience. Watch them and talk to them. Mix with them sometimes off duty. Give them a party now and then. Listen to them, not to eavesdrop, but to understand, by learning the random careless rhythm of their chatter, how their emotions and minds really work. But as well as doing this, you can learn a great deal about them by remembering your own youth. The more intensely you can think yourself back into those parts of it which seem farthest away from your present adult life, the better you can understand the young. Some of the least successful teachers on general work are men and women who, even when they were boys and girls, had an air of premature solemnity and un-childlike primness, who studied hard and seldom played rough or silly games, and whose parents kept them in cotton-wool. Often they enjoyed themselves best, not as boys among boys, or girls among girls, but when assuming the teacher's authority and omniscience. Such youngsters often earn good marks, and then shrink from going out into the rude world to make a living by adventurous competition. Then they take up teaching as a career, and are surprised when they dislike so much of it. Sometimes, however, they are extremely good with bright, hard-working boys and girls who remind them of themselves. They project all their ambitions on to such pupils, training them to get good scholarships and pass difficult examinations. But they are rarely much good with the ordinary youngsters who fill the average class, because they themselves have never been either ordinary or young.[5]

The art of teaching the child is unique in many dimensions. The modern teacher is best justified in teaching children when she/he no longer remains the so-called teacher but enriches herself/himself as a learner-friend, learner-sister/brother, learner-companion and learner-assistant. The more she/he creates a natural and joyous teaching-learning environ for children, the more is education for fullness.

Are we prepared to translate our conjoint and communicated promises and priorities in child education?

REFERENCES

1. Stella Vasniadou: *How Children Learn,* UNESCO, 2001, pp. 18-19.
2. "Learning and Knowledge", *National Curriculum Framework 2005,* National Council of Educational Research and Training, New Delhi, 2005, pp. 30-31.
3. *Ibid.,* p. 90.
4. Sri Aurobindo: "Education of the Child", *Education and the Growing Child,* Sri Aurobindo Institute of Research in Social Sciences, Sri Aurobindo Society, Pondicherry, 1996, pp. 4-5.
5. Gilbert Highet: "The Teacher", *The Art of Teaching,* Methuen, London, 1963, pp. 33-35.

2

COMMUNICATION EDUCATION: SETTING NEW AGENDA OF MOTIVATION

Education is primarily meant for development of the mind and the heart. If the mind suffers from absence of development in the right direction under right climate of efflorescence contributing to ascent and excellence, the purpose of education in the true sense of the term is to a great extent dwarfed and defeated. Simultaneously, if education fails to ignite the finer sensibilities of the mind that embolden the heart not only to sustain but also to enrich the superior ends-in-view of life, it loses its inherent worth as an inseparable and unparalleled guide and guardian of fullness of human worth. It is, therefore, absolutely necessary that education cares for and is concerned with diverse and definite plans and programmes of teacher and pupil motivation, motivation of administration and supervision notwithstanding, in communication education.

What is really embarrassing in communication education is that despite motivation plays a very significant role in it either directly or indirectly, the identification of the different nuances of motivation leading to interest, skill, attitude, aptitude, comparative analysis, differentiation, synchronisation and appreciation, leaving aside the obligatory standpoint of accessibility and understanding, is alarmingly absent from practice and execution. The results are as follows:

(*a*) Theories and principles are given unusual importance.
(*b*) Bookish education becomes very prominent.

(c) Information allows no room for entry into the world of intensive and in-depth communication.
(d) Artificial and mechanical strategies of teaching and learning become the hallmark of communication education.
(e) Dullness and drabness in communication education call forth unwelcome and derogatory recess of and absence from imaginative thinking.
(f) Absence of creative and critical thinking eats away the essence of education in and through excessively routine-rolled communication studies.
(g) Too much of activism tells upon alertness and dynamism necessary for spontaneity and clarity of vision.
(h) Freedom of mind and heart received and exercised through a healthy and absorbing climate of natural and interactive motivation in communication studies.
(i) Education of human rights under straight-jacket and/or manipulated communication devices demotes quality and advancement in education.
(j) Education of good citizenship sans priorities and progress in well-defined motivation programmes under communication studies becomes an absolute myth.

Setting new agenda of motivation in communication against all constraints in communication studies as above necessitates our sincere attention to the following objectives:

(a) To create a sound and effective teaching-learning environment for exercise of motivation in communication studies.
(b) To enable the teacher and the learner to exercise the finer components of motivation to accelerate and improve the quality of education imparted and/or received.
(c) To identify and introduce the most significant and appropriate strategies of motivation cues, hints or suggestions as and when necessary for worthwhile communication.
(d) To locate the finer and delicate constraints in practice

of motivation so that communication becomes meaningful, pointed and transparent.

(e) To accelerate the plus points of motivation for better and more advanced strategies of communication.

(f) To intensify more inquisitive and attractive process of motivation geared to and pregnant with the inputs of communication as a natural and spontaneous means of desirable and characteristic efflorescence of humane inter-relationship.

The Three-Fold Strategy

Setting new agenda of motivation for excellence in communication education look forward to introducing the three-fold strategy that highlights clarity, patience and responsibility. For clarity, the teacher is equipped with the following:

(i) firmness in resolution,
(ii) simplicity in choice of words,
(iii) accessibility for the learner,
(iv) ability to put inside the learner's mind,
(v) stress on probing matters of delivery,
(vi) introducing apposite illustrations,
(vii) opening challenging avenues of interactions, and
(viii) introducing prompt and pregnant subject-matters of allied interest.

For patience as one of the most successful strategies of communication education, the following are considered important:

(i) providing a learner with sufficient time for involvement in communication education through a self-styled but appropriate motivation outcome,
(ii) introducing, analysing, evaluating and enriching teacher-pupil interaction,
(iii) allowing sufficient scope for enrichment of discussion through motivation,
(iv) turning informatics into reflections in crystallised thoughts received from various ends,

(v) controlling the irregular and irrelevant motivation cues, and

(vi) arresting emotions as and when motivations of the right kind and also of the right order demand.

The important principle to be carried out in education for communication enriched in motivation is responsibility on the part of the teacher in particular. It is crucial to achieving perfection in communication that the teacher motivates in the correct and scientific way. As Gilbert Highet characteristically observes:

> It is a serious thing to interfere with another man's life. It is hard enough to guide one's own. Yet people are easily influenced for good or evil, particularly when they are young or when their teacher speaks with authority. The effects of bad teaching, of glib and shallow advice, of money-grubbing or publicity-hunting declarations to a trusting public are quite incalculable. Every now and then the papers mention that a man has been arrested for selling a Cancer Cure composed of bread pills flavoured with saccharin. He gets ten years; but how can that compare with the tortures he has inflicted on his "patients"? In the same way, it is hard to see how any politician who has once offered to teach the public what was right on a vital issue, and who has been proved wrong, can ever venture to open his mouth again. But they are seldom punished, and sometimes praised as versatile and constructive thinkers. It must be a fearful thing to write a series of plays and novels, rapidly and irresponsibly, in order to gain a reputation and make money; and then, late in life, to realise that they express foolish or wicked ideas, and to be ashamed of your own words. The surest safeguard against that is to ask how your ideas could possibly be misused or misunderstood, and to think, not of yourself, but of your friends and brothers whom you are trying to teach.[1]

Indeed, communication education always looks forward to creating a favourable climate of motivation for the learner so that at least three principal purposes are served. First, the learner finds that the lesson to be learnt does not make him/her passive and disinterested. Second, the content is well within his/her solid grip for transaction and transmission, recall and retention as and when necessary for further attention. Third, the motivation that he/she receives can be well-diverted towards meaningful transfer of learning.

With a view to negotiating the motivational dimensions as above, the teacher should create an atmosphere of positive thinking amongst students. This means that motivation no longer becomes an aid to learning alone but it boosts individuality. The students become conscious of their own inner strength and weakness as well to form their own propositions for transparency in thought and action. This is where the role of the teacher as an appropriate and judicious person in providing feedbacks, cues, hints and suggestions can hardly be averted. A good teacher knows very well when and how feedbacks can enrich motivation. Accordingly, all instructions prompt and motivate learners to engineer and utilise their willpower with rational and reflective thinking.

Setting a new agenda of motivation in and through communication, therefore, requires a vibrant role of the teacher in motivating pupils to exercise their unique willpower. The five major areas of motivation in this regard are:

1. Identification of the nature of pupils' willpower.
2. Analysis of the vulnerable areas of the pupils' willpower.
3. Relational components.
4. Ends-in-view of willpower.
5. Reflective and probing perspectives.

To be justified to the five major areas as above, the teacher strategies of motivation may vary from student to student under myriad learning atmosphere. As motivation in communication education in accelerating and implementing willpower is crucial to effective teaching, the teacher must plan and organise stimulating avenues of development. In this connection, the suggestions put forward by Boekaerts are very significant and noteworthy:

> How can you help your students to develop willpower? First of all, you should not be misled by observed effort. When effort investment is high (or low), you still need to know why that is the case. In order to be able to interpret student initiative, persistence and disengagement meaningfully, you need to have a good idea of the way your students perceive the learning goal and also of how much effort they need to invest to reach it. Students should be given plenty of opportunities to practice striving for goals. You can coach this process by reminding them to set a series of sub-goals and to compose a checklist that will help them to monitor, assess and reflect on the quality of their engagement and commitment during the solution process.
>
> Reflecting on the goal-striving process implies that students should raise questions about the resources that are necessary and sufficient to reach the various sub-goals. For example, Stefano may ask himself: "Do I have sufficient time to finish my history homework before dinner if I reread every section twice and make a brief summary?" Post-activity reflection about effort-investment is essential to make students aware of their attempts at effort management and of the reason why they did not exercise willpower. By asking your students to compare and contrast the amount and type of effort invested in various tasks, you can help them to develop their theory of effort, and at the same time allow them to gain insight into their own willpower.[2]

The methods of teaching for motivation in communication education cannot remain methods only. These vary from a teacher's own motivation maps controlled or free in a classroom or elsewhere. The students know and learn effectively when matters are communicated in precise and pointed order. At the same time, probable communication gaps are also taken into serious consideration under motivation perfection.

Therefore, the methods are to be applied in response to pupil-motivation where communication must be very clear, purposeful and, over and above, enriched and resourceful. The teacher must be well aware of the fact that the art of good questioning wins the mind of the learner where communication fulfils its very crucial initial role. The technique of questioning leads to ignite motivation which, again, leads to the end-in-view of desirable and worthwhile communication. As Highet advises:

> Never underestimate the power of a well-put question to illuminate the darkness. Students who have been passively absorbing information and allowing it to trickle out almost as fast as it was poured in will often come to life and take an active interest in their work when questions start flying. But the real value of the question-period at the end is for the conscientious students. It is worth while to read through a lecture-notebook kept by a student of good intelligence and industry. The gaps and misunderstandings in it will astound you. Often these youngsters are afraid to ask you to fill in the gaps, because they do not want to give themselves away. They think you will snub them, or answer perfunctorily. If you do, you are committing a crime. Instead, you should make it easy for them to ask for corrections, full names, the exact figures, the complete references. Don't simply wait for them to demand help. Offer it. You have not always spoken clearly. Foreign names and complex formulas are difficult to write down quickly. A cough will cover up half a vital sentence; and, in many cities now-a-days, at least five minutes of every hour's teaching is made inaudible by the roar of transport aircraft apparently flying just above the roofs. The last few meetings of the class are your opportunity to wash away all that mud, and reveal your own lost pearls.[3]

The knowledge and skill of the teacher in synchronic with the curriculum to be enacted by the teacher educator with its scheduled programme of strategies are all guided by motivation. The interactions that take place among the teaching-learning clientele are to be reoriented in tune with the defence mechanism of motivation. This means that good motivation should be given further fillip while undesirable and bad motivation should either be brushed aside or tailored to the needs of qualitative ends-in-view of advancement in education. Professor Kelley explains this very adroitly in dealing with student achievement from the standpoint of improvement by means of undertaking a thorough check in policy and performance in leadership strategies:

> Internal accountability systems include both formal and informal aspects. An example of formal accountability is an evaluation system linked with performance expectations. Informal accountability includes the things that teachers hold themselves accountable for (individual responsibility) and the things that teachers hold one another accountable for (collective responsibility) within the school.

Together, teacher knowledge and skills, teacher motivation, and situation influence the extent to which the *enacted curriculum* will be effective at producing student achievement. Student achievement takes place through the enacted curriculum, which is the series of interactions between teachers, students, and the curriculum that occur over time. What students learn depends not only on the curriculum, but on the way that the teacher understands, interprets, and presents that material, and the attitudes and previous knowledge that the student brings to a series of teaching moments (Cohen & Ball, 1998). Thus, a student's knowledge of writing (for example) depends on a series of interactions between curriculum, teacher, and student over time. The artistry in producing excellent writers through policy is in cutting through the layers in the system enough to influence the ways in which teachers and students interact with curricular materials. Because teaching and learning are highly engaging tasks, these influences must be internalized by teachers so that they consciously influence curriculum and instructional decisions, and so that they influence the ways that teachers and students interact at a subconscious level as they engage in learning.[4]

Motivation in communication education is like a fine tapestry. It should be so well-knitted in the strategies of education as to arrive at meaningful interaction and purposeful pupil achievement. Therefore, all policy makers, management and leadership from educational administration and curriculum negotiation points of view. As Kelley adds:

> The artistry in weaving a policy tapestry is in combining policy, leadership, and management at the state, district, and school levels to create the knowledge and skills, motivation, and context that will result in meaningful interaction between teachers, students, and instructional materials in the teaching moment. This is why it is so difficult to make a policy that has a clear effect on student achievement. Assuming that policies themselves are well-designed (which can be a problematic assumption given the politics of policy formation), policies must not only *penetrate* administrative layers, but district management must reinforce, accommodate, and not conflict with these policies; and teacher knowledge and skills, motivation, and school context must support policy implementation so that teachers purposefully and effectively incorporate these policies into their teaching practice, and internalize them enough to draw on them while engaging with students in the enacted curriculum.[5]

In communication education, the strategies for pupil motivation should admit two significant points of reality: one, creating a set pattern of pupil understanding and expression oral and/or written, and the other, pupil disinterestedness in process-oriented feedback. If these two major areas of deficiencies are negotiated in an ambience of sincerity and steadfastness to acceleration of motivation in a positive and sympathetic understanding of the major issues therein, education and success become a thrilling reality. In order to create favourable motivational beliefs that ensure and facilitates vibrant teaching learning climate, intrinsic motivation should be the end-in-view. As it is not always possible even in triggering self-determination in every student, the emulating inroads may be switched over as and when necessary. As Boekaerts characteristically observes:

> Unfortunately, not all students are intrinsically motivated and you also have to cater to those students who are less motivated to learn. It is important to realize that classroom climate and the way you interact with your students facilitates or impedes their motivation. Try to make tasks and activities meaningful for your students by referring to the intrinsic values of the task and to potential applications in other subject areas and outside school. How can you help your students to develop favourable motivational beliefs? Translate the curriculum in terms of the skills that your students find relevant and interesting. Find out what their current interests and future career goals are (e.g., Sandra wants to become a nurse and Stefano wants to become a space engineer). Show a video, a newspaper cutting, or tell a story, highlighting the importance and functional relevance of new content and skills. Ask students who are already motivated to explain why they value these new skills. Alternatively, ask your students to interview their parents, other teachers in school or older students to find out when they use the new content or skills. These activities will catch your students' attention and curiosity. This is already half of the motivation story. The other half is holding their interest. It is important that students perceive an optimal match between perceived demands and their current capacity. Allow them to adapt exercises according to their current capacity. For example, Stefano gets bored when math problems are too easy. Do not force him to cover the content of the lesson at the same pace, or in the same way, as the slower learners. Also, encourage students to find out a math

problem too demanding, to redesign it in such a way that it becomes less threatening (e.g., Sandra: 'Can I do this math problem together with Claudia?'). Allowing students to adapt a learning activity to their own psychological needs gives them a feeling of autonomy and self-determination. Denying them this right will be interpreted as external pressure to comply.[6]

The world of communication education is stimulating and challenging from the different unexplored areas of motivation. It is a world where all avenues of communication are rich in diverse components of learning and teaching. While the students are always at crossroads with unusual stints of motivation, teachers are also curious to find out the permissible inputs of learners to be in perfect tune with what they learn out of their own responses to whatever means of communication they negotiate. Let us reschedule our programmes of communication education mapping the most vulnerable areas of motivation so that the whole programme of teaching becomes lively and thrilling, adventurous and pulsating in translating joy and freedom in education.

REFERENCES

1. Gilbert Highet: *The Art of Teaching*, University Paperbacks, Methuen, London, 1963, pp. 247-48.
2. Monique Boekaerts: *Motivation to Learn*, International Academy of Education, UNESCO, 2002, p. 21.
3. Gilbert Highet: *The Art of Teaching*, University Paperback, Methuen, London, 1964, pp. 148-49.
4. Carolyn Kelley: "From Policy to Performance: Weaving Policy and Leadership Strategies to Improve Student Achievement", *Educational Leadership: Policy Dimensions in the 21st Century*, Bruce Anthony Jones (Ed.), Frank Bros. & Co. Noida, India, 2000, pp. 78-79.
5. *Ibid.*, p. 79.
6. Monique Boekaerts: *Motivation to Learn*, UNESCO, 2000, pp. 12-13.

3

ACCELERATING QUALITY IMPROVEMENT IN COMMUNITY MOBILISATION: AESTHETIC PARAMETERS

Education is crucial to the creation of a new and altogether challenging ascent and excellence of humans. This is all the more viable and forceful in education for community development in order to translate the ends-in-view of Sarva Shiksha Abhiyan.

How to make education viable and forceful? How, again, to make it apposite so that the members of the community are really and worthily justified to and judicious for the all round improvement of quality? As a matter of fact, community mobilization essentially precedes the promise and poignancy of quality improvement in diverse programmes on Sarva Shiksha Abhiyan and this cannot but be conscious of how to highlight, orient and disseminate the aesthetics of quality education in all earnestness and accuracy, involvement and spontaneity. Undeniably, SSA in absolute unison and efflorescence of aesthetic sensibilities ensures education for fullness.

Bearing in mind that a community anywhere and everywhere should be consonant with the formal and the functionally aesthetic components of a group of people living together and sharing the advantages and disadvantages, weal and woe, vision and reflection under a conjoint and communicated atmosphere, the success of Sarva Shiksha Abhiyan greatly depends on how the members of the community are equipped with the aesthetic education of the heart—the education that is always in quest of the excellence of all the finer qualities and softer visions of life. Hence, the importance of quality improvement through training programmes for the members of the community.

Admittedly, one of the principal spell-outs in the definition of Sarva Shiksha Abhiyan is 'a response to the demand for quality basic education all over the country', and unless an aesthetic awareness to undertaking and involvements of the different members of the community associated directly or indirectly with the Panchayati Raj Institutions, Mother Teacher Associations, School Management Committees, Village and Urban Slum Level Education Committees, Tribal Autonomous Councils and similar other grassroot level organisations in management, supervision and advancement in elementary education spontaneously and vigorously take place, the mission of Sarva Shiksha Abhiyan would not be meaningful, life-centric and vibrant for an emerging and ever-enlightened India.

Community based monitoring of training in aesthetics should always be conscious of implementing package training programmes for active participation of the members of the community where one of the fundamental objectives of Sarva Shiksha Abhiyan namely, 'focus on elementary education of satisfactory quality with emphasis on education for life' is not only ensured but also effectively manifested by means of cultivation of lifelong and serene aesthetic values. Even the private schools failing somehow or other to be justified to promoting Sarva Shiksha Abhiyan right now demands a warm welcome to the great but arduous and challenging task of universal retention by 2010 which is not very far. In fact, training programmes for community members should be geared to the vital area of exploring newer directions of public-private partnership in Sarva Shiksha Abhiyan where the aesthetic components to be exercised and oriented for enrichment and stabilization of quality is guaranteed in all-embracing community mobilization.

Thrust Areas

Prior to launching any training programme for the members of the community in translating the ends-in-view of Sarva

Shiksha Abhiyan into a real success in life and work, the following thrust areas necessitate sincere and dynamic attention:

(a) Identification of the vulnerable areas of aesthetic education to be imparted by means of text matters for Sarva Shiksha Abhiyan.

(b) Preparing text matters especially with a view to inculcating aesthetic values amongst the learning clientele.

(c) Explaining the spirit of different aesthetic components with careful and cautious emphasis on how to translate them in personal and social day-to-day activities and involvements.

(d) Stimulating individual and creative endeavour in consolidating education in terms of aesthetic refinement geared towards networking national and global aesthetic consciousness.

(e) Addressing the socio-cultural ethos and moorings where the inherent spirit of Sarva Shiksha Abhiyan is well-nourished by continual and sustained aesthetic advancement and excellence.

(f) Setting newer agenda for Sarva Shiksha Abhiyan in terms of the most prized aesthetic sensibilities translated in all earnestness towards education for fullness.

To organise training programmes for the members of the community under the ambience of the District Education Programme schemes especially geared towards fulfilment of the objectives of Sarva Shiksha Abhiyan in aesthetic poignancy and efflorescence in catholicity, the following areas of activities with micro-level spell-outs under different educational climate necessitate our sincere attention and involvement:

I. The Early Phase

At this stage, the trainees as members of the community should undergo training programmes on the fundamental aesthetic components that play a very significant role in quality acceleration in the teaching-learning schedule of activities. So far as imparting instructions to the learners are concerned, these aesthetic components can be exercised and cultivated in two ways: external and internal. In the day-to-day teaching-learning process, the role of the trainee-members of the community in the operational strategies of Sarva Shiksha Abhiyan should at first exercise the aesthetic components externally because this would lead to attention, interest and stabilization of internal aesthetic components. For example, the aesthetic component 'beauty' can very well be exercised through learning how to decorate the classroom or any other place in the altar of learning by *alpana-s*, using leaves, flowers and foliages for learning, in addition, the aesthetic quality of simplicity. This may be further extended for exercise of the aesthetic components like grace, naturalness and elegance through use of flower garlands, hats, bangles, ear rings made of bamboos, use of sandal paste, incense, earthen lamps—all absolutely indigenous but remarkably aesthetic and symbolic of finer artistic sensibilities and softer visions of life. As regards teaching and training of external aesthetic sensibilities, one can very well spell-out charity, magnanimity, kindness, truth, service, humility, righteousness and many other socio-cultural and socio-aesthetic values by identifying, presenting, applying and evaluating amidst diverse community climate available or likely to be available under a heterogeneous fusion of rural-urban-slum learning set-up that calls forth setting newer and more pin-pointed agenda of training programmes for the members of the community.

II. The Middle Phase

At the very outset of this stage, three different but in the final analysis a single unit in oneness of the quality-effulgent stages of aesthetic sensibilities should come under the purview of any effective training programme for the community members to translate Sarva Shiksha Abhiyan into a success in all elegance and perfection. These are:

(i) *The Incubation Stage:* This stage is crucial to the natural and smooth exercise of aesthetic components that are

the positive outcome of the groundwork of aesthetic qualities exercised at the early stage. This may not be available at the early stage of exercise in some cases where the role, for example, of Early Childhood Care and Education (ECCE) or Integrated Child Development Service (ICDS) or any other allied organizations/ institutions are some how or other constrained in discharging their duties and responsibilities in the best possible ways as consolidated and conjoint partners to quality assistance and enrichment in Sarva Shiksha Abhiyan. But these can be successfully negotiated by organising additional and/or sandwiched programmes followed by intensive refresher course training and orientation ones.

(ii) *The Illumination Stage:* For effective exercise of quality in aesthetic sensibilities, this is perhaps the most important stage. The members of the community under the training programme should be so oriented as to be justified to the following:

(a) the major components contributing to the right manifestation of illumination of aesthetic sensibilities,

(b) the minor components of aesthetic efflorescence under constraints consequential to adverse community climate,

(c) the total inputs of aesthetic communication,

(d) the probable direct and/or indirect outcome of aesthetic exercise,

(e) evaluation of aesthetic illumination in terms of quality assurance and advancement,

(f) identification of the desirable avenues of transfer of training in aesthetic illumination,

(g) verification of intra and inter community interactions and handling of teaching-learning materials for positive aesthetic outcome in training and orientation, and

(h) dealing with evaluation on the basis of verification as above.

(iii) *The Post-Illumination Stage:* It is also called the stage of perfection in poignancy of the aesthetic components for quality enhancement and accreditation. At this stage the four fundamental areas of quality mobilization of aesthetics earmarked for dynamic training programmes should be taken into urgent and serious consideration for sustenance and further enrichment of quality education for all:

(a) active and vibrant participation of all members of the community encompassing VECs, Panchayats, MTAs, PTAs and others complimenting to the success of education at the grassroot level,

(b) sensitizing quality education in aesthetics by prioritizing community-based and monitored training programmes by means of introducing micro-planned teaching-learning activities leading to welcoming and negotiating pitfalls of learners with different abilities in a heterogeneous community complex,

(c) evolving work-prone short-term/long-term/ intensive modules and packages for training for more exciting avenues of exercise in aesthetics which would assimilate, internalize and keep pace with the rapid progress of mass media programmes of Sarva Shiksha Abhiyan, and

(d) arranging seminars, symposia, and workshops on quality mobilization of aesthetic sensibilities for the trainee-members of the community as well as for the trained-experts who would also undergo intensive pre-service and in-service programme in order to be better equipped with newer strategies of dealing with Sarva Shiksha Abhiyan on a war footing.

III. The Final Phase

This phase is the phase of integration of all evaluation outcome under the different objectives of Sarva Shiksha Abhiyan. This is always challenging and demands an in-depth vision of education for fullness in the mission of education for all.

The following is a network of the whole training programme for catering to the needs and priorities for effectively sensitizing aesthetic development through Sarva Shiksha Abhiyan:

> What is greatly needed is a conjoint approach to introducing the most essential aesthetic qualities under training programmes so that successful implementation in Sarva Shiksha Abhiyan leads to education that appositely responds to the emerging and vital needs of the country. Involvements of the community in effective guidance, supervision and monitoring of Sarva Shiksha Abhiyan under integrated programmes of action also demand upgrading of standard in aesthetic sensitization where Alternative and Innovative Education (AIE) well synchronized with Education Guarantee Scheme (EGS) contributes a lot to minimizing ukase in the planning process of primary education and especially education for out-of-school children at both the upper and the lower primary levels.

If 'All learn, all advance' as the mission statement of Sarva Shiksha Abhiyan is to be a vibrant reality, scientific and systemic networking of training programmes for community members in every nook and corner of the country will have to be introduced with greater and more enlivening utilization of academic personnel especially the retired senior citizens for more quality training in aesthetic sensitization.

Catch-now Areas

The catch-now areas under the training programmes on aesthetics in Sarva Shiksha Abhiyan for the community members may be identified as follows:

1. Orientation programmes on the essentials of aesthetic education at the elementary stage.
2. Survey and planning for detailing out activities thereto.
3. Phased involvements in the training schedules.
4. Spelling out vulnerable areas of action.

5. Introducing refresher course programmes on quality enhancement in aesthetic education.
6. Networking integration avenues for consolidation of aesthetic sensibilities introduced and exercised, analysed and evaluated.
7. Guidance and research activities for the members of the community to erase out constraints in the quality acceleration programmes on Sarva Shiksha Abhiyan.

And Miles to Go

Unlike any other adventure in exploring newer horizons of education, it is high time to translate the ardent aesthetic mission of Sarva Shiksha Abhiyan as the flagship programme par excellence of reaching the ends-in-view of Universalization of Elementary Education (UEE). At the same time, it is also desirable that UEE always upholds and disseminates the perfumes, as it were, of education for poignancy and elegance by highlighting quality acceleration in aesthetics amongst everyone in tune with the spirit of advancement. Why not launch aesthetic education for effective community awareness and mobilization in the training and orientation programmes on Sarva Shiksha Abhiyan which has already invited the world of digital divide in quest of ascent and excellence in education?

4
EDUCATION FOR PROBING INTO THE LEARNERS' WORLD: SOCIO-AESTHETIC DIMENSIONS

When Education truly becomes learners-friendly, it serves its purpose best. It looks forward to creating a typical world for every learner who naturally becomes self-interested, self-motivated, self-appreciated, self-apprised and, above all, self-taught and self-learnt. As a consequence, the teacher relegates herself/himself into the background with the most desirable prize of teaching for fullness as the enviable dividend.

Admittedly, teaching is a conjoint experience where group instruction is certainly necessary for two very crucial constraints in the family where the learner more often than not is vulnerable to indiscipline and absence of the qualities of sociability. But that must not be allowed to predominate, as it is the cruel and in some cases unavoidable fact, over efflorescence of individuality. Who ignores the best role of the teacher who always succeeds in making an apposite fusion of individualising instruction with socialising the child?

Socialisation right now ought to be geared towards exploring newer avenues of how to receive the best out of teaching for competency-enhancement and quality-acceleration of every learner. Unless the teacher is well-acquainted with the unique world of the latter's world of learning, keeping in view how to be in perfect tune with the inner world of learning through probing and illuminating interactions, perhaps learning takes its back seat and teaching turns out to be an abstraction and mechanical exercise.

Care for the learners' world, therefore, contributes a lot to quality teaching. It primarily calls forth three most essential components spelt out as follows:

First, a true teacher is a continual and innovative learner. The learning takes place as soon as she/he directly and/or indirectly associates herself/himself with students. In case of direct association, she/he ardently plays the role of a learner-assistant, learner-partner and learner-follower as and when necessary. This provides positive opportunities for detailing, motivating, probing and appreciating the matchless world of the learner along with her/his own learning as a teacher. This ultimately shows the way of excellence in teaching-learning where freedom is exercised in a favourable manner and joy pervades in all spontaneity. In the direct association with the learner as it is always desirable, the teacher has endless opportunities for having a judicious entry into the four areas of the learners' world of learning, which is symbolised in questions:

(i) Are the learners really motivated in learning?

(ii) What are their constraints in openness of creative and aesthetic efflorescence?

(iii) What cues, hints and suggestions are necessary for addressing their manifold and diverse world of anticipation, illumination and exposition?

(iv) What should be the real plans and programmes for teaching for having a conjoint and communicated experience in startling nuances of aesthetics exercised or likely to be exercised as a definite outcome of quality education?

Second, as a social agent for quality education, the teacher has the arduous but thrilling task of preparing each learner to be justified to be logical, scientific, creative, critical and innovative as best as possible. This pre-supposes the former to be well-acquainted with the latter's world of learning in freedom and joy, spontaneity and curiosity. It is the proper role of the former to be very intimately associated with the latter's world of the processes and strategies of learning, more interested in the latter's trends and tendencies of progress and decide and introduce strategies of teaching. Otherwise the learner's world would be very much ignored and the purpose of good teaching would be severely affected.

Third, every learner, by virtue of her/his age, intelligence, interest, attitude and sense of appreciation, frantically seeks her/his world of learning to be emotionally nursed and accelerated. Naturally, her/his aesthetic sensibilities like truth, beauty, goodness, love, sympathy and many other finer visions of life look forward to sincere involvement both in theory and practice with a careful and cautious approach to subjectivity. It is no wonder that a little bit of the teacher's own aesthetic sensibilities serenely administered in a cordial manner work wonders in probing into the aesthetic world of the learner. In fact, an experienced and controlled teacher knows that teaching aesthetics is actually showing the probable avenues and never teaching as such.

The techniques of teaching for probing into the world at the early stage demand greater attention and involvement. These include some of the fundamental ends-in-view of socio-aesthetics as follows:

(a) To enable the learner to go ahead with his concepts and experiments of socio-aesthetic sensibilities with close and intimate cooperation received from teachers in different subjects or on different items of learning as and when necessary.

(b) To encourage the learner to be more self-assertive, self-supportive, self-confident and self-advanced through enrichment of knowledge and experience either by self-study or by self-experimentation, where the aesthetic sensibilities are identified and exercised in an incomparable and unparalleled manner.

(c) To stimulate the essential components of socio-aesthetic visions of life with a positive sense of value awareness and value culture.

(*d*) To encourage comparative studies on different components of socio-aesthetic patterns of behaviour both in theory and in practice.

(*e*) To cultivate the finer nuances of social and aesthetic designs of efflorescence with a singular bias of points of manifestation in order to strengthen and enrich individual socio-aesthetic marvels of advancement.

(*f*) To promote a favourable socio-aesthetic school-society relationship in advancement of learning.

(*g*) To accelerate a greater and more intensive world of teacher-pupil socio-aesthetic fusion of mind.

The discovery of the wonders of the world of socio-aesthetics inherent in every learner is a very challenging task. While content-competency is undeniable, methods and techniques of introducing the finer concepts of socio-aesthetics amongst learners with individual differences in legion should be so relevant, fool proof, pin-pointed, precise, distinct, arresting and stimulating that these are not only endeared by them but also treasured and revised in accordance with their own tastes and temperaments as and when necessary. Sometimes these techniques are introduced just to ignite the learners' awareness to socio-aesthetic traits of personalities, and the rest automatically follows. The learner discovers her/his own world of aesthetics where she/he is allowed to exercise and enjoy how to uphold and enrich worthwhile social ways and means of life with a tinge of more delicate and softer issues and feelings.

Indeed, one of the best ways to probe into the learners' world as a teacher is to allow every learner to chalk out her/his own world of socio-aesthetics and never thrust their own ideas, concepts, imagery-patterns and so on to be belittled or dwarfed or even challenged. It is belief—positive belief, of course—in the learners' kingdom of knowledge and experience that outshines the broadened vision of socio-aesthetics of the former. And therein is enshrined the grand success of the method of teaching. As Gilbert Highet characteristically suggests:

The best way to avoid wasting the powers of a good pupil is to plan his work for him. You need not necessarily tell him that it is all laid out some distance ahead. Better not. Sometimes that discourages him. But you must arrange matters so that, at the end of a three-month or a six-month period, you will be able to make him look back over the journey he has made and be pleased and surprised at its extent. Make him keep records. Make him write. Extract from him groups of notes on the successive experiments he makes, or get him to put down a weekly summary of the period he has been studying, or set him a series of essays carefully designed to guide him through every sector of an important field. Then, at the end of three months, give him a rest and congratulate him, and while he is still elated, take him rapidly over his whole achievement. This gives him a sense of unexpected power; fixes the broad outlines of his work much more firmly in his mind; allows bold general ideas time to germinate on him; and often stimulates him to suggest further work in a direction that would not have occurred to you. It is also valuable insurance against those fits of depression that often afflict the brilliant. When he comes to you haggard and sullen after being baffled by a new set of problems, and says he is convinced all his effort has been wasted, then you will produce the solid collection of work he has already done, show him how far he pushed ahead during that period, persuade him that his profits there are inalienable, and, if you feel it wise, explain how the present period of work will dovetail into the earlier. Usually he will appear unconsoled. The young are easily changed, therefore, they like to pose as being immutable. But after going away he will look back over the immediate past—his own, hand-made, unique, indestructible past, the work that has become part of himself—and he will start again with new energy to hammer out his future.

Such pupils you must know. You must know the geniuses, the loonies, and the weaklings—all the eccentrics. You must know some of them for your own protection—in the same way as a wise physician with a new paranoiac patient telephones his previous doctor to get a complete history of his weaknesses and treatment. Others you must learn in order to draw the maximum out of them and put the maximum in. the rest, the typical students, you need hardly know as separate persons.

But—one last word—never let them feel that they are only types: that would be quite wrong. If they ask for personal advice, it is your duty to give it freely and pleasantly. If they have special inclinations, they will be delighted to hear you discuss them. You should not, however, feel it your responsibility to know every single one of your pupils as well as you know the special individuals whom we have been discussing—since average youngsters, being easier to educate in a class and more friendly to the rest of their group, do not need such particular attention.[1]

Teaching with a sense of humour well-directed towards the will-force of the learners in delving deep into the world of softer feelings and sentiments not only harbours success of a very high standard but also promotes an ambience of right thought expressed and applied in the right pattern with the right effulgence of inwardness. In fact, an intensified aura of teaching-learning makes teaching all learning for the teacher and, alternately, learning all teaching in a synergic pattern by the learner.

To be a teacher par excellence in probing into the learners' world of socio-aesthetics is to be without being a bandwagon of erstwhile ideals and practices. Classrooms can be anywhere. These can, alternately, be nowhere. As aesthetics is everywhere as societies are existent, the platforms of teaching can be identified, located, set, designed and experimented in tune with the needs and possibilities of pupil-motivation. Let the learners' world be anywhere and everywhere. Let the fire of aesthetics ignite their minds just as it ignites or compels to ignite their teachers as well to make a conjoint adventure in teaching-learning.

Exploring worthwhile mechanisms of sensitisation in socio-aesthetics calls forth a warm welcome to tutoring. This is a term more often misused and diluted than not, thanks to misguided socio-economic viewpoints and explanations. Let us, as teachers, reduce talking and increase more facilities for inviting and receiving responses from learners. Let every tutee be allowed to devise her/his unique strategies of negotiating the world of learning. In this connection, the practical suggestions put forward by Topping as follows contribute a lot to socio-aesthetically compliment better education in and through tutoring in teaching:

Avoid Lectures

Do not give tutees long, complicated explanations. Keep everything short, to the point and in simple words. Give positive instructions for what to do. Do not emphasize what *NOT* to do. If necessary, explain again briefly, but in different words.

Review

Often it is helpful to briefly review what you learned in your previous tutoring session.

Concentrate

Stay focused on the task in hand. Do not drift off into irrelevant conversation. Tutoring time is precious. Use it well. But have some fun while learning.

Variety

Mix up easy and hard tasks; short and long; highly structured and open-ended; talking, reading and writing.

Question

Don't just ask for a fact or one-word answer. Ask questions that are open-ended and encourage the tutee to talk. But do not make them too complicated. Ask questions that make the tutee think and reveal their understanding (or misunderstanding). Ask questions that make the tutee apply, analyse, predict, classify, synthesize, justify or evaluate what they are learning. Some of these questions will have more than one 'right' answer. Do not accept guesses.

Thinking Time

Do not expect the tutee to respond to a question immediately. They will need some thinking time. Tutors can give them that, while school teachers cannot.

Prompt

Do not just tell the tutee the answer. Give them a small clue about how to work out the right answer. This might be drawing or a gesture (for example), as well as more spoken words. Give just enough support to enable the tutee to be successful with some effort—no more.[2]

To educate children to be worthy of and justified to what they think and act, imagine and accomplish is to allow them to be justified to the immediate society to which they belong and to which their grooming in aesthetic sensibilities is successfully directed. As a matter of fact, the curriculum should be so designed and implemented as to enable them to exercise their aesthetic fineness in all freedom and spontaneity, joy and curiosity. Every society looks forward to the education of children to be geared to that very direction which inspires the learners to respond to their inner beckoning of aesthetic fulfilment. It is for this very reason that concern for quality in education calls forth curriculum reform in the national framework:

> Curriculum reforms are at the heart of any wide-ranging initiative that may be taken to improve the quality of educational provision at different stages. The prevailing curricular reality needs to be addressed in the following terms:

> The tendency to confuse knowledge with information must be curbed. The tendency encourages the transfer of topics from higher to lower levels.

Treatment of children's learning as an isolated outcome should be replaced by the application of developmental norms that assume a holistic pattern of growth in motivation and capacity.

Productive work needs to be viewed as a pedagogic medium for knowledge acquisition, developing values and multiple-skill formation from the pre-school to the senior secondary stages.

Curricular choices have to be made with due regard to the child's context, ensuring the flexibility and diversity of the approaches emphasised in NPE-1986 and POA-1992.[3]

To probe into the learners' world is to delve deep into the teachers' world of looking within and looking for the long lost but ever green memories of childhood. The old familiar faces of childhood ought to be revived for the sake of doing justice to every child who is like the blackbird always seeking the prize for self-expression. One cannot deny the spirit of adventure in learning by each and every child in accordance with his/her tastes and temperaments in quest of the best out of his/her knowledge and experience, understanding and skill, interest and attitude, aptitude and the overall power of synchronised appreciation.

For new frontiers of education, education of the child should prove its genuine urge for efflorescence of the child who actually learns not from his/her teacher but from his own inner response. In this connection, the following words on the role of new education as 'a new attitude towards the child' would definitely serve as a milestone in exploring new frontiers of education:

> New education ....is really a new attitude towards the child. An attitude of understanding and love, and above all an attitude of respect. An attitude of

> expectation, of patience; the restraint of a delicate hand that dare not open a flower-bud nor disturb a baby in the midst of his first experiments, a student in the course of his early work. ....

The child has within himself everything that is necessary for a true education, and particularly a ceaseless activity, incessantly revived, in which he is totally engrossed, the activity of a growing being who is continuously developing and to whom, for that very reason, our help may be useful, but our direction is not necessary.[4]

To probe into the learners' world as a teacher is to be assured of planning every lesson she/he imparts. The sense of purpose in teaching is very crucial and it must be well spelt out and manipulated in worthwhile dimensions for the best outcome in the learners' probing. As Highet characteristically observes:

> One of the chief aids to learning is the sense of purpose. One of its chief rewards is the sense of achievement. One of its chief aims is to develop the structural faculty, which in intellectual matters shows itself as foresight and co-ordination, and in art gives the appreciation of harmony and the power to create it. The teacher should have all these in view as he prepares his work. By example and by practice, he can show the young that it is a weakness to live from day-to-day, and that accumulation and planning mean strength.

The best way to do this is to plan all the work which the class will do, to explain the plan to them, to make sure that they keep it in mind, and, after the work has been completed, to look back over it and sum it up. The young have very little ability to make long-term plans. They live from day-to-day, or at best from one Saturday to another. Teachers are sometimes infected by this malady, or take advantage of it, to save themselves the trouble of planning and the effort of sticking to the plan. They are sometimes apt to devote the term to reading one textbook, to studying one branch of their subject, and to let themselves drift week by week, carried on only by the flow of historical dates, the succession of chapters. Although this feels easier, it is vastly more tedious for their pupils, and even for themselves.

**** **** ****

Each class should therefore be given, before it starts work, a summary of the ground it will cover. Some teachers merely talk about the main outlines of their subject. Others dictate a neatly arranged programme, paragraphed and sub-paragraphed. Others hand out a typed leaflet, containing the main topics which will be discussed, arranged not week by week but in their logical order, so that the student can see their internal connections, prepare questions on subjects that interest him particularly, and, if he has been absent, find out what he missed. For the humanities—art, literature, languages, philosophy, history, politics—it is a little discouraging to have the work sliced up and packed into airtight compartments, each containing one week's ration. It is better in these subjects to allow the teacher and the class scope to develop their discussions without being kept to a time-table. It is the logical structure of the work that should be prepared and made known. In the sciences, and in law and medicine, it is probably better to maintain a suitably exact time-plan.[5]

The world of aesthetics is the world of beauty, truth, goodness, love, joy, modesty, patience, simplicity and many other values that adorn a living and loving society. Transfer and transparency of all these make education meaningful and dynamic, fruitful and all-embracing in the society. When economic challenges are at every point of our social development, education for probing awareness to aesthetic development in terms of 'discovery and experiment' in creative and aesthetic development contributes to all other dimensions in humane development. As the Report to UNESCO of International Commission on Education for the Twenty-first Century significantly suggests:

In an ever-changing world in which social and economic innovation seems to be one of the main driving forces, a special place should doubtlessly be given to the qualities of imagination and creativity, the clearest manifestation of human freedom, which may be at risk from a certain standardization of individual behaviour. The twenty-first century needs this variety of talents and personalities; it also needs the exceptional individuals who are also essential in any civilization. It is therefore important to provide children and young people with every possible opportunity for discovery and experiment—aesthetic, artistic, sporting, scientific, cultural and social—as well as appealing introductions to the creations of their contemporaries or earlier generations. Art and poetry, too often taught in a way that has become more utilitarian than cultural, should again be given more importance in schools than is commonly the case in many countries. The desire to develop the imagination and creativity should also result in higher regard being paid to oral culture and knowledge derived from the child's or adult's experience.[6]

Do we sincerely adhere to the above?

REFERENCES

1. Gilbert Highet: *The Art of Teaching,* Methuen, London, 1963, pp. 47-48.
2. Keith Topping: *Tutoring,* UNESCO, 2000, pp. 11-12.
3. *National Curriculum Framework 2005,* National Council of Educational Research and Training, New Delhi, December 2005, p. 102.
4. Roger Cousinet: *L'Education Nouvelle,* Delachaux et Niestle, Neuchatel & Paris, 1950, pp. 20-21.
5. Gilbert Highet: *The Art of Teaching,* University Paperbacks, Methuen, London, 1963, pp. 69-70.
6. *Learning: The Treasure Within,* UNESCO, 1996, p. 95.

5

EDUCATION AND CONSTITUTIONAL PROVISIONS IN HUMAN RIGHTS

Education is a significant component and contributor to promotion and excellence in human rights. It caters to individuality and at the same time makes a characteristic development of human behaviour with enrichment in design and efflorescence, democratisation and excellence. As a matter of fact, education becomes truly operational and meaningful when its primary concern for protecting, nourishing and disseminating the essence of human rights is judiciously dealt with under myriad and challenging circumstances.

The National Human Rights Commission in its specification of the Human Rights Act, 1993 has categorically emphasised on the right to education and pointed out the importance of exercising that right for appropriate human resource development. In defining the Functions of the Commission, the following have been clearly spelt out:

(a) inquire *suo moto* or on a petition presented to it by a victim or any person on his behalf, into complaint of

- *(i)* violation of human rights or abetment thereof or
- *(ii)* negligence in the prevention of such violation, by a public servant;

(b) intervene in any proceeding involving any allegation of violation of human rights pending before a court with the approval of such court;

(*c*) visit, under intimation to the State Government, any jail or any other institution under the control of the State Government, where persons are detained or lodged for purposes of treatment, reformation or protection to study the living conditions of the inmates and make recommendations thereon;

(*d*) review the safeguards provided by or under the Constitution or any law for the time being in force for the protection of human rights and recommend measures for their effective implementation;

(*e*) review the factors, including acts of terrorism that inhibit the enjoyment of human rights and recommend appropriate remedial measures;

(*f*) study treaties and other international instruments of human rights and make recommendations for their effective implementation;

(*g*) undertake and promote research in the field of human rights;

(*h*) spread human rights literacy among various sections of society and promote awareness of the safeguards available for the protection of these rights through publications, the media, seminars and other available means;

(*i*) encourage the efforts of non-government organisations and institutions working in the field of human rights;

(*j*) such other functions as it may consider necessary for the protection of human rights.[1]

The functions of the non-government organisations and other institutions devoted to encouraging and disseminating education in the field of human rights are legion. These functions are primarily two-fold: immediate and long-term. The immediate functions cater to the propagation of human rights and, for that end-in-view, identify, analyse and implement those rights by means of manipulating education in the apposite direction. For this, identification and management of manpower potential especially designed for the purpose of meaningful and purposeful response to the salient points of human rights are absolutely necessary. So far as the long-term functions are concerned, education should be equipped with several course structures where planning and organisation of activities related to betterment of standards of living, refinement of good sense and sensibilities, respect towards every citizen anywhere and everywhere with human rights cultivated and caressed in all serenity and catholicity play a very vital and worthwhile role in human resource development.

Education for promotion of human rights necessitates a strong theoretical foundation for which the essential prominent areas of human resource development should be properly identified, classified and translated into action. The broad-based theoretical areas should include the rights of children as the main focus of attention because education should be concerned with that of the rights of children at the outset.

The rights of children to learning include the right of being a real partner to national development and enrichment of human worth. For this, the right to live and enjoy living and growing as a child with assurance and translation of satisfactory growth and development is the obligatory end-in-view of education.

The fundamental aims and objectives of education of the child as an inevitable function for translation of human rights are as follows:

(i) To enable every child to learn in a natural and enviable atmosphere of freedom and joy of living.

(ii) To ensure every child to have nutritious food for a sound health complimenting worthily to have a sound mind.

(iii) To provide every child with a healthy and convenient climate of education.

(iv) To safe guard every child from forced involvement in earning and employment in lieu of freedom and joy in learning.

(v) To guarantee regular medical check-up, treatment and medicine, nursing and convalescence facilities for children free of cost for children.

(vi) To fillip the innovative and inquisitive qualities of children at every step of incubation, development and illumination.

(vii) To create a cordial relationship between the child learner and the teacher so that independent exercise of curiosity and joy becomes natural and spontaneous.

(viii) To arrange for generating a healthy spirit of exercise of creativity and aesthetic sensibilities by warding off mechanical, dull, drab and routine-oriented academic and allied activities for children.

(ix) To accelerate motivational avenues in conformity with children's temperaments and potential aspirations to learn and practise as best as possible.

(x) To provide children with ample opportunities for probing into the different plans and programmes of activities self-directed or guided by teachers, parents, guardians, communities etc.

The education of the girl child as a very important arena of human rights hardly needs any special mention. In particular, it may, however, be mentioned that the constitutional provision of safeguarding and enriching education of the girl child awaits more consolidated, positive and penetrating approach. The right to grow up and develop personality as an essential and obligatory component of human right is yet to be given its appropriate importance. Lack of public awareness, passivity in community consciousness and, over and above, indifference to decent living besides malnutrition, partisan approach to negotiate the inward quest for fullness in gender-free education terribly tell upon right to education of the girl child. With increasing violence, sexual or otherwise, the dawn of a new era of mass awareness to education in this direction has been camouflaged in social habits, manners and customs rampantly observed and illegally thrust upon girls so much so that the right to nurture freedom and individuality is continually constrained in utter callousness. The right to eradicate apathy and ignorance by means of introducing and highlighting the major issues and possibilities of the education of sympathy can no longer be forcefully delayed. The more the right to education of the heart is disseminated in keeping with equalisation of opportunities for all, the more would positively be the definite and genuine outcome of implementation of human rights.

The right of the old and senior citizens to be honoured in the society and to be provided with essential opportunities like food, medicine, health care and co-operation depends almost entirely upon how education is best geared towards the right to introduce, restore and enrich perennial social, aesthetic and cultural values of India. As the Upanishad says, *matrideva bhava, pitrideva bhava, acharyadeva bhava,* let the education of understanding and appreciating senior citizens become a solid and paramount foundation of human rights. Again, let research on values old and new with a sustained approach to re-establish the missing links of sensitised and serene education abundantly ensure crystallised education of human rights.

Education for good citizenship as an important component of enrichment of personality should come under the purview of better organisation of human rights. There is no denying the fact that the right to decent living as a free citizen is not yet given appropriate attention even in theoretical dimensions, practice in day-to-day activities in educational institutions notwithstanding. The right to decent living demands the education of the heart where the aesthetic components of living and loving are not only learnt theoretically but also exercised practically in course of leading daily life. It includes a psychological foundation as well where motivation takes a very important role. The education of human rights for decent living, therefore, is primarily motivational from three important perspectives. First, this right takes care of what is good to humans and eliminates the harmful and dangerous components of irresponsible and selfish living in the patterns of passivity, indifference, egoistic tendencies, truancy, absence of righteousness, magnanimity and broader or more glorious visions of life like self-sacrifice or reducing oneself to a cipher. At the same time, the right to be educated with the higher spirit of altruism delivers humans from self-mockeries and diverse forms of littleness like absence of conjoint and communicated, shared and sympathised living. Unless education for awareness to human rights especially in the aesthetic and spiritual dimensions is well-ventilated by means of meaningful and worthwhile motivation, education and human rights altogether remain prisoners of alienation. In the world of today what is urgently required for dynamic and vibrant education is to explore and execute diverse avenues of motivation in teaching and learning that bring forth a better canvas of catholicity of vision in all-endearing education.

With promises and poignancies in highlighting and crystallising education in terms of constitutional provisions in human rights, ensuring, encouraging and stimulating genuine autonomy for educational institutions in resource management encompassing negotiation, collaboration and a healthy spirit of cooperation with all agencies private or public are obligatory. Let all doubts and discrepancies be eliminated and a conjoint and solid approach to enliven human rights through and in education become a living reality.

Undoubtedly, human rights await opportunities for proper realisation and manifestation. This is why education in schools in this direction should take the pivotal role in tune with autonomy in human rights programmes of action. As the Delors' Commission rightly suggests:

> There are various aspects to schools' autonomy. It applies first to resource management: the school should be able to decide how to use a substantial portion of its allotted resources. Ad hoc bodies, such as committees composed of parents (or pupils) and teachers, can in some cases be set up to advise on school management and the curriculum. More generally speaking, there should be procedures in each school for defining the role of all the parties concerned and promoting co-operation among teachers, school principals and families, as well as broader dialogue with the community. The practice of negotiation and collaboration where school management and school

life in general are concerned is in itself a democratic learning process. The autonomy of educational institutions also strongly encourages innovation. In over-centralised systems, innovations tend to be confined to pilot projects which, if successful, are meant to give rise to broader measures. These are, however, not necessarily relevant to every situation. There seems to be wide agreement that innovations depend largely for their success on local circumstances. It may, therefore, be more important to propagate the capacity for innovation than to disseminate the innovations themselves.

The Commission favours a broad decentralisation of educational systems, based upon school autonomy and the effective participation of the local stakeholders. The need for an education pursued throughout life and the emergence of learning societies using the resources of informal education should, in its view, accentuate this trend. It is at the same time aware that methods of educational organisation and management are not ends in themselves but are instruments whose value and effectiveness depend largely on their political, economic, social and cultural context. Decentralisation measures can form part of a democratic process or, equally well, of authoritarian processes leading to social exclusion.[2]

The constitutional provisions in education for advancement of human rights await a more specific spell out in better strategies for exploring newer avenues of marriage between centralisation and decentralisation in every item of interest in education. Care should be taken to generate the principles that ensure right to promote socialisation without sacrificing the prospects, priorities and translation of individuality under transfer of learning and transparency.

For a participatory democracy, education should ensure the right of every child to nurture development of a conjoint voice in the great spirit of oneness. As the National Curriculum Framework (NCF) significantly elucidates:

> India has signed the Convention on the Rights of the Child (CRC). The three most important principles of this Convention are the rights to participation, to association or the right to organisation, and the right to information. These are essential rights if children and youth are to realise all their other rights. CRC does not concern itself only with the protection of children and the delivery or provision of services and programmes, but also ensure that children have the right to determine the quality and nature of these services and programmes. Moreover, all the articles of the CRC have to be seen within the overarching principle, that of upholding and preserving the best interests of children.

Although CRC guarantees children the right to express their views freely in all matters affecting them, and to exercise freedom of expression, children are frequently denied the opportunity to participate in decision-making processes and activities that effect their lives and futures. The right to participation also depends on the realisation of other primary rights such as access to information, the freedom of association, and the right to formulate opinions free from influence and coercion. The principle of participation should be integrated into all areas of concern for children.

In reality, social, political and economic structures are still very much hierarchical; children and youth are the most marginalised sections of society; their effective participation depends largely on the extent to which they are given the opportunity to organise themselves. Coming together gives them visibility, strength and a collective voice. The participation of individual, 'hand-picked' children or youth is fraught with discrimination, and is ineffective because such 'representatives' represent no one but themselves; it excludes the less vocal and less visible, and it gives more room for manipulation.

On the other hand, the organised participation of children and youth, especially the more disadvantaged children, gives children strength, access to more information, confidence, an identity and ownership. Individual children or youth representing such groups voice the views and aspirations of the collective. Their coming together also enables them to find collective ways to solve problems. However, what needs to be ensured is that all children and youth have an equal right to participate in the development of this collective voice.[3]

The education of children should also guarantee the right to study in their own languages in which they are brought up in their own home environment. The right to be educated in the mother tongue is always a plus point for learning in joy and freedom, and it should be free from all encumbrances. At the same time, the role of parents and community should always be supportive to the right of every child to enjoy a favourable learning environment in every school. The suggestions put forward by the NCF in this connection are as follows:

The participation of the community in the child's world of education and learning should allow for the community to:

(a) Transfer oral history (dealing with folklore, migration, environmental degradation, traders, settlers, etc.) and traditional knowledge (sowing and harvesting, monsoons, processes related to traditional crafts, etc.) to children, while the school encourages critical reflection wherever it is required.
(b) Influence the content of subjects and add local, practical and appropriate examples.
(c) Support children in their exploration and creation of knowledge and information.
(d) Support children in their practice of democracy through their participation in information generation, planning, monitoring and evaluation with local governments and schools.
(e) Monitor the realisation of children's rights as well as violation of these rights.
(f) Participate in addressing the constraints faced by children.
(g) Participate in setting criteria for vocational training.

(*h*) Enable the village to become a learning environment for children realising the concept of the 'village as a school'.

Similarly, while helping children to use their home language and make a transition to the school language, teachers may seek inputs from local language speakers to facilitate communication in the mother tongue(s), teaching of languages and creating material. The choice would depend upon the particular curricular plan adopted and the kinds of expertise that are available and accessible. The school must explore opportunities for active engagement by parents and the community in the process of learning. This relationship will help in sharing the content and pedagogy of institutional learning.[4]

The right to create a living institution for children demands the right to have a perfect and learner-teacher-society friendly environment. Parental right to have their children to be gifted with an ideal environment where learning is a way of life itself must be ensured. Local communities and organisations should also come forward to look into every aspect of children's right to be educated in the most successful pattern under a convenient climate of advancement.

As regards, the learning materials for children, a fresh look is right now necessary or never. Children have the right to deal with best books, best maps, drawing materials, paper, pen, pencil etc., unfortunately, this area is not given desirable importance. The right to be the users of best learning materials for children promises better efflorescence of child personality—a fact which requires greater attention and interest in every educational institution.

For a newer vision of national and trans-national consciousness for quality education, constitutional provisions of human rights demand a separate approach to ensure child education not merely in exercising universal, free and compulsory but at the same time taking a more challenging venture in freedom and joy in learning as a spontaneous response from every child rural or urban, poor or rich, advantageous or disadvantageous, normal or otherwise able. Let a new provision of constitution be framed where the voice of children about their joy and freedom, agonies and sufferings, sorrows and misfortunes find a direct platform of expression. Let every child open out the heart within. Let a new frontier of the lotus land of excellence emerge in teaching and training in child education based on rights, duties and responsibilities.

Are we right now ready for a new dawn of consciousness for the education of the child in perfect symphony with the constitutional provisions of human rights?

REFERENCES

1. "Human Rights Act 1993", *National Human Rights Commission,* New Delhi, Chapter III, pp. 5-6.
2. *Learning: The Treasure Within,* UNESCO, 1996, pp. 159-160.
3. *National Curriculum Framework 2005,* National Council of Educational Research and Training, New Delhi, 2005, pp. 84-85.
4. *National Curriculum Framework 2005,* National Council of Educational Research and Training, New Delhi, 2005, pp. 88-89.

6

EXPLORING QUALITY IN CHILD EDUCATION: AESTHETIC AVENUES

Education is a challenge. Quality education for children is a greater and more arduous challenge because it calls forth more intensive and in-depth vision of askance and enquiry, critical and aesthetic exercise. As a matter of fact, the child fails to be blessed with the ignition of aesthetic manifestation not because it is not receptive to the nuances of aesthetics awaiting efflorescence in unique brilliance but essentially because it is deprived of a favourable climate of learner-teacher thrilling interaction.

Apart from the fact that the teacher speaks more than the child in the classroom which more often than not betrays freedom in learning by the latter, it is unfortunate that the former pays little attention and interest in better individualization of instruction in the plea of the so-called socialization of the latter. The result is appalling because neither the learner nor the teacher is justified to education for excellence.

How to be justified to excellence? How to be in perfect tune with the learner in the classroom or elsewhere inside or outside in the pursuit of education? All these and similar queries look forward to making a continual and sustained adventure into the world of aesthetics. The strategies for this end-in-view are not regimented. Instead, these are wide open and subject to variations as and when necessary. The mind of a child is always eager to respond to any item of learning that never compromises with abject and inane commonality. What Rabindranath Tagore refers to as freedom and joy in learning without being captivated and dwarfed by the so-called teacher who has very little to teach but very much to be branded as a pre-historic enormously figured animal is the fountain of quality effulgence in education of the child. Moreover, it is not desirable to arrest education in the rigour of any syllabus that knows no compromise with time, work like a hydraulic pressure, to appositely coin the words of Tagore, and build the careers of children, the would-be citizens as proxy-prone 47A or 69E of *Red Olienders.* What a catastrophe in the name of quality in child education!

With the challenges in child education in the backdrop as above, let us launch radical agenda in quality education through aesthetic advancement with the following ends-in-view:

(i) To enable every learner to be christened in the world of learning where freedom and joy are natural and spontaneous.

(ii) To stimulate the learner that in the process of learning there is no alternative to creativity and critical thinking at any stage of learning anything whatsoever and howsoever.

(iii) To fillip every learner to be as justified to her/his aesthetic consciousness to the best of her/his abilities.

(iv) To direct the learner to be inspired in her/his plus points of quality exercise in aesthetics and enhance more enriched effulgence, and, simultaneously eliminate the minus points that stand in the way of appropriate exercise of aesthetic sensibilities.

(v) To prepare every learner to identify the most salient components of learning that necessitates intensive aesthetic involvements for quality acceleration and orient the strategies to be negotiated for finer efflorescence of aesthetic illumination.

(vi) To reduce unnecessary learning components in the best interest of the learner whose strategies of learning should be allowed to enjoy warmth of positive support by the teacher who would try as far as possible to

provide her/his pupil with fool-proof, pointed, significant and worthwhile cues, hints or suggestions as and when required, and relegate herself/himself to the background.

(vii) To provide the learner with positive aesthetic climate of quality advancement in learning and act as a learner-assistant in both theory and practice of performance.

(viii) To explore the finer components of the learner's aesthetic sensibilities which promise a living fusion with imageries, linguistic stylistics, expressional points of excellence and, above all, consolidation and poignant presentation of aesthetics in quality assured creative grandeur.

(ix) To verify the loopholes in the process of the learner's aesthetic exercise and, since they are very delicate, sensitive, relational and soft, suggest similar or allied avenues of quality manifestation in the light of the learner's attitude, aptitude, appreciative designs, taste, temperament and skill in the exercise under consideration.

(x) To make the learner interested in penetrating studies of her/his own aesthetic exercise by means of self-analysis and self-evaluation side by side with a thorough understanding, appreciation, interaction and follow-up programme for quality acceleration.

The Four E-s

Child education for quality teaching to be justified to aesthetic development is a highly sensitive and innovative activity which calls forth the serene role of every teacher. Here she/he is not only a hard task master but quite interestingly and, of course, spontaneously an aesthetic creator-assistant whose involvement as a partner acts as an enzyme to the learner's aesthetic endeavour. In fact, in the ardent endeavour of entering into the cathedral of perfection in aesthetic exercise both the learner and the teacher enjoy the same platform of quality illumination where appreciation is shared and shouldered, conjoint and correlated with vision of oneness in perfection, convergent for the time being notwithstanding.

Of the four E-s that pave avenues of quality assurance of aesthetic development in child education, encouragement comes first. If the learner child is encouraged in education from the aesthetic points of view, she/he will definitely find an altogether new ambience of learner-friendly subjective advancement where reasons are refreshed in aesthetics and quality is resonant with pregnancies of thoughts and experiments well-nourished in creative and critical thinking. That a child never knows any failure in her/his trillion-dollar ambitious adventure in the world of learning, promises the fact that a little bit of encouragement acts as an ever-boosting stimulant.

The second E from the teacher's end towards the child learner for quality nourishment in aesthetics is elucidation. It is a highly delicate component of aesthetic exercise where a little bit of departure from the sense of propriety and proportion may deliver disaster to aesthetic construction of quality citadel. Every child has infinite possibilities of how to build up her/his own selected aesthetic patterns of thoughts and ideas to be developed in all artistic fullness in creativity. Under the circumstances, if the teacher identifies and enriches her/his learner's own strategies of aesthetic exercise and judiciously manipulates elucidation accordingly, well and good. If not, who can arrest massacre in teaching and fail to ditto with the Shakespearean outcry: 'Mischief, thou art afoot'?

Erudition is the third E which is a characteristic and essential component. It guarantees and protects quality from de-standardization. It demands devotion to the extent of reducing oneself to a cipher in terms of recognition to every child learner's unique and incomparable aesthetic genius. In fact, it is to every teacher's infinite amazement that very often the child learner is far ahead of her/his normal aesthetic appreciation to what the experts fail to identify and interpret and this is clearly evident in synchronizing diverse imagery patterns in the most skilful and intrinsic manner so much so that we ignorantly take these for others' contributions and not her/his own, very much own and original. Now, if the child finds her/his teacher as a friend, comrade and peer, what a joyous and living atmosphere in education for fullness in aesthetic appreciation and serenity! When would our altars of learning be qualified and accelerated in building such cathedrals of carefree, colourful, conscious and conjoint contours of aesthetic illumination?

Excellence, the fourth E, is, let us frankly admit, waning in an alarming manner, thanks to education that even now fails to avert education that is satisfied with how to get something or simply work-crazy education—in the words of Tagore, *kichhu paiye debar siksha* or *kejo siksha*. Under such circumstances, one cannot but absolutely bid farewell to quality education through cultivation of aesthetic sensibilities. In extra-super craziness for caressing carcass of our very existence by muttering "We have no time to stand and stare," we agonizingly recall Eliot's askance: "Where is the life we have lost in living?" Unless excellence is prioritized in teaching, children would be the worst sufferers. For this, the teacher requires training and orientation in the essentials of aesthetic education. Seminars and workshops on aesthetics in quality identification, analysis and assessment would also assure promotion of excellence in teaching.

In the 'design and development of the curriculum and related matters' on quality enrichment in teaching for aesthetic fullness, the role of nature can hardly be ignored. One might recall Amagi's invaluable words in this connection:

> Teaching methods, textbooks, teaching materials and aids should be developed at the same time as the curriculum. * * * *Academic research developments in natural and social sciences, and humanities should be taken into account in curriculum development. The important role of experimental studies, and experience of working and living with nature, should also be considered in the development of teaching and learning methods.[1]

To explore newer avenues of quality in child education, motivational avenues should be greatly checked in full consonance with the evaluation patterns that are framed in tune with pupil-attitude to learning. In fact, the design and the lunching of assessment should be carefully scrutinised beforehand and newer strategies for such ends-in-view should be crystallised in terms of transparency and quality assurance in being justified to every learner. The physical and psychological stress consequential to competition in the name of identification and evaluation of quality should be appropriately arrested. As it is significantly highlighted:

> The types of questions that are set for assessment need to go beyond what is given in the book. Often children's learning is restricted as teachers do not accept their answers, if they are different from what is presented in the guidebooks.

Questions that are open-ended and challenging could also be used. Designing good test items and questions is an art, and teachers should spend time thinking about and devising such questions. The interest and ability of teachers to design good questions can be promoted through district or state-level competitions. All question papers must be designed, graded for difficulty in order to permit all children to experience a level of success, and to gain confidence in their ability to answer and solve problems.

Trying to devise a good and effective open-book examination can be a challenge that we must try to take up in our curricular efforts at all levels of school. This would require teachers and examination setters to emphasise the interpretation and application of learning over the arguments and facts that can be located in the book. There have been successful demonstrations that such examinations can be carried out on a large scale, and that teachers can themselves be trusted with moderating the results of such examinations. In this way, the assessment of projects and lab work can also be made credible and sound.

It is important that after receiving their corrected papers, children re-write the answers and that these are again reviewed by teachers to ensure that children have learnt and gained something out of the ordeal.

Competition is motivating, but it is an extrinsic rather than intrinsic form of motivation. It is, of course, much easier to establish and to manipulate, and therefore frequently resorted to by teachers and school systems as a way creating and nurturing the drive for excellence. Schools begin 'ranking' children as early as their pre-primary years as a way of inculcating in them a competitive spirit. Such a competitive drive has several negative side effects on learning; often superficial learning is sufficient to create and maintain impressions, and over time students lose their ability to take initiative or do things for the fulfilment of one's own interest; hence, areas that cannot be 'marked' are neglected. This has unhealthy consequences for classroom culture, making children individualistic and unsuited to team work. There is an absurd and unnecessary importance given to term examination, often accompanied by extreme arrangements of invigilation and secrecy. While the physical and psychological effects of this may not be readily visible until middle school, they frequently lead to high levels of stress in children, and cause early burn out. Schools and teachers need to ask themselves whether there is really much to be gained out of such practices and to what extent learning requires such systems of marking and ranking.[2]

For the Delight of the Perfume of Promise

Teacher education for exploring quality in aesthetic education will all the time have to undergo strenuous and valiant challenges. But the ever stimulating promise of perfection beckons and, indeed, beckons with an aura of illumination. Meanwhile, let us attune ourselves with the incomparable aesthetic resonance and serenity of Tagore:

> This is my delight, thus to wait and watch at the wayside where shadow chases light and the rain comes in the wake of the summer.

Messengers, with tidings from unknown skies, greet me and speed along the road. My heart is glad within, and the breath of the passing breeze is sweet.

From dawn till dusk I sit here before my door, and I know that of a sudden the happy moment will arrive when I shall see.

In the meanwhile I smile and sing all alone. In the meanwhile the air is filling with the perfume of promise.[3]

REFERENCES

1. Isao Amagi: Upgrading the quality of school education, *Learning: The Treasure Within,* UNESCO, 1996, p. 200.
2. *National Curriculum Framework 2005,* National Council of Educational Research and Training, New Delhi, 2005, pp. 74-75.
3. Rabindranath Tagore: *Gitanjali,* Macmillan India Limited, New Delhi, Macmillan Pocket Tagore Edition, 1983, XLIV, p. 26.

7

EDUCATION OF THE FUTURE: SRI AUROBINDO'S VISION

Education is what one ought to be for what one is. To Sri Aurobindo, it is more than what one ought to be. It is ascent beyond ascent in and through excellence beyond excellence. As such, education of the future calls forth evolution of consciousness that paves for the lotus land of the unison of the being and the Super Being, the grand vision of the Rose of God.

Education of the future as Sri Aurobindo envisions in all purity and perfection, is an assured transition from the Mind to the Supermind. This calls forth embracing reality in terms of the aesthetic culture of Truth, Beauty and Goodness. A study of knowledge or intellect should never end in or be rest assured with, as it normally does, its fulfilment or success which often remains incomplete or fractional. In fact, knowledge is the primary step of enriching two other vital objectives. These are education of the heart or what is generally identified as the education of the best exercise and efflorescence of emotion, and that of the action or will which denotes responding to the future of humans. Sri Aurobindo emphasises on a spontaneous, regular, systematic, disciplined and harmonious blending of knowledge, emotion and action that consolidates and guarantees education of the future.

Admittedly, education of the future as Sri Aurobindo envisions and translates into reality is a definite pointer and promoter of withdrawal within for a bold response to the call of the beyond. It is the central being within everyone that looks forward to becoming a pathfinder to the emergence of man, the exponent of the true Soul. Education of the future cannot, therefore, ignore transformation and transcendence in terms of all-endearing divine realisation. It is time to uphold, enrich and empower education that brings about a radical change as an opener to the world of the Infinity of Consciousness, All-Power and a limitless Self.

What Sri Aurobindo advocates as new consciousness in and through education is to welcome and exercise incomparable and unparalleled forces of thought and sight in every individual. Feeble we often are due to lack of, or, more assuredly, absence from cultivation of exercise of spiritual realisation that crystallises our thought and sight. How to treasure the depth of vision in education that promises continual refinement of all our contemplation and action? To answer, Sri Aurobindo suggests for the culture of the Supermind. This necessitates education as a vehicle for transit, external as well as internal, from Mind to Supermind. And, for this, the unlimited powers of the Super-conscious should be explored unendingly so that each and every person is sincerely uplifted and elegantly transformed in course of cultivation of the mind from four positive points of queries. First, is education a promoter from the lower mind to the Higher Mind? Second, does it enable transfer and transcendence from the matter-of-fact mind to the Intuitive Mind? Third, does it lead to illumination prior to intuition? Fourth, does it equip the mind as the Supramental Force so that everyone becomes the ideal being of human unity, the spiritual man par excellence?

As a unique visionary of the Spiritual Age, Sri Aurobindo advises for a radical movement in education and society from matter to Spirit. In his own words:

> If mankind is to be spiritualised, it must first in the mass cease to be the material or the vital man and become the psychic and the true mental being. From this point of view, it is a sign of great promise that the

> wheel of civilisation has been following its past and present curve upward from a solid physical knowledge through a successive sounding of higher and higher powers that meditate between Matter and Spirit, with a large but swift evocation of each level.

The true secret can only be discovered if in the third stage, the idea becomes strong of the mind itself as no more than a secondary power of the Spirit's working and of the Spirit as the original and the sole reality. Then only will a spiritual age of mankind become possible, which would start from and realise three essential truths of existence which are as yet for the mass of mankind only words and dreams,—God, freedom and unity, three things which are one.[1]

To be justified to the spiritual age of mankind as Sri Aurobindo unfolds, education of the future cannot but be an unending endeavour at the pure, serene and perfect consummation of the spiritual man. This is the Supramental or Gnostic being who for the freedom of the spirit strives for the education that welcomes the transcendent aspect of spiritual life. How to christen our children right from the beginning of their pursuit in education? How to administer moral training for them through education so that each one of them responds to his/her inner voice of the wholeness and the beyonding of consciousness? Sri Aurobindo's suggestions are very poignant and significant:

> The first rule of moral training is to suggest and invite, not command or impose. The best method of suggestion is by personal example, daily converse and the books read from day-to-day. These books should contain, for the younger student, the lofty examples of the past given, not as moral lessons, but as things of supreme human interest, and, for the elder student, the great thoughts of great souls, the passages of literature which set fire to the highest emotions and prompt the highest ideals and aspirations, the records of history and biography which exemplify the living of those great thoughts, noble emotions and aspiring

> ideals. This is a kind of good company, *satsanga,* which can seldom fail to have effect so long as sententious sermonising is avoided, and becomes of the highest effect if the personal life of the teacher is itself moulded by the great things he places before the pupils. It cannot, however, have full force unless the young life is given an opportunity, within its limited sphere, of embodying in action the moral impulses which rise within it. The thirst of knowledge, the self-devotion, the purity, the renunciation of the Brahmin—the courage, ardour, honour, nobility, chivalry, patriotism of the Kshatriya—the beneficence, skill, industry, generous enterprise and large open-handedness of the Vaisya—the self-effacement and loving service of the Sudra— these are the qualities of the Aryan. They constitute the moral temper we desire in our young men, in the whole nation. But how can we get them if we do not give opportunities to the young to train themselves in the Aryan tradition, to form by the practice and familiarity of childhood and boyhood the stuff of which their adult lives must be made?[2]

An exalted education of the future in terms of the above as Sri Aurobindo envisions is again possible in India and the world at large only when it will ensure our children to be capable of learning, opening, absorbing and engaging their entire being in the perfect mastery of knowledge that makes a symphony of the voice of the Vedic saints and seers and the most profound scholars in supercomputers of the modern era. Moreover, a quest for the honour of education as the fountain of love recognised and endeared by the radical immediate and distant community is yet to be undertaken as a promise to be translated into action right now for a vibrant future. Where is a genuine response to the evolutionary movement of the heart? When would education be a serene vehicle for reviving and regenerating the soul of the *Visvamanav*?

Truly, it is time to celebrate the coming of the subjective age. For this end-in-view, education in general and of the child in particular should explore thrilling avenues of cultivating newer visions and possibilities in order to ensure the progress of humans and civilisation. As Sri Aurobindo reminds us:

> The individualistic age, proceeding by individual mind and reason, however, must go from the individual to the universal. In Europe in modern times that has taken the form of physical science. But after a time it must become apparent that this is not the whole knowledge; that man is a mental as well as a physical and vital being. Therefore to find the truth of things and the law of his relation to that truth he must go deeper and fathom the subjective secret of himself and things. This he may attempt to do for a time by the power of critical and analytical reason, but not for long. For in his study of himself he cannot but come face to face with the soul in himself and the soul in the world and find it to be an entity so profound, so complex and so full of hidden secrets and powers that his intellectual reason betrays itself as an insufficient light and fumbling seeker. All those tendencies are manifest in the world today. The art, music and literature of the world have also undergone a profound revolution in the direction of an ever-increasing subjectivism, from the vital to a mental, intuitional and psychic, pointing to the direction in which the human mind is being piloted on a momentous voyage of discovery. This can be seen also in the new ideas about education and upbringing of the child.[3]

For a new age to be born, the children of the future begin education in the sound backdrop of refinement of subjectivity. This is a modest beginning for providing the required passage to the efflorescence of 'the potentialities of a deeper self-discovery' continual and painstaking, yet adorable and challenging.

The role of the teacher in the education of the future is legion. Observe and concentrate, involve and evolve—these are the positive guidelines for children in living and wholesome education. The invaluable words of Sri Aurobindo on the duties and responsibilities of the teacher are profoundly significant:

> Almost every child has an imagination, an instinct for words, a dramatic faculty, a wealth of idea and fancy. These should be interested in the literature and history of the nation. Instead of stupid and dry spelling and reading books, looked on as a dreary and ungrateful task, he should be introduced by rapidly progressive stages to the most interesting parts of his own literature and the life around him and behind him, and they should be put before him in such a way as to attract and appeal to the qualities of which I have spoken. All other studies at this period should be devoted to the perfection of the mental functions and the moral character. A foundation should be laid at this time for the study of history, science, philosophy, art, but not in the obtrusive and formal manner. Every child is a lover of interesting narrative, a hero-worshipper and a patriot. Appeal to these qualities in him and through them let him master without knowing it the living and human parts of his nation's history. Every child is an inquirer, an investigator, analyser, a merciless anatomist. Appeal to these qualities in him and let him acquire without knowing it the right temper and the necessary fundamental knowledge of the scientist. Every child has an insatiable intellectual curiosity and turn for metaphysical enquiry. Use it to draw him on slowly to an understanding of the world and himself. Every child has the gift of imitation and a touch of imaginative power. Use it to give him the groundwork of the faculty of the artist.[4]

Servation in the education of the child takes a very prominent role. The ideal teacher knows how to create interest in the child so that he/she can develop his/her faculty of observation in tune with Nature. What is required on the part of a teacher is to teach the child in developing his/her instruments of knowledge, feelings and imaginations with utmost clarity and thoroughness, sincerity and prudence. Sri Aurobindo characteristically elucidates:

> The first qualities of the mind that have to be developed are those which can be grouped under observation. We notice some things, ignore others. Even of what we notice, we observe very little. A general perception of an object is what we all usually carry away from a cursory half-attentive glance. A closer attention fixes its place, form, nature as distinct from its surroundings. Full concentration of the faculty of observation gives us all the knowledge that the three chief senses can gather about the object, or if we touch or taste, we may gather all that the five senses can tell of its nature and properties. Those who make use of the sixth sense, the poet, the painter, the Yogin, can also gather much that is hidden from the ordinary observer. The scientist by investigation ascertains other facts open to a minuter observation. These are the components of the faculty of observation, and it is obvious that its basis is attention, which may be only close or close and minute. We may gather much even from a passing glance at an object, if we have the habit of concentrating the attention and the habit of sattwic receptibility. The first thing the teacher has to do is to accustom the pupil to concentrate attention.

We may take the instance of a flower. Instead of looking at it and getting a casual impression of scent, form and colour, he should be encouraged to know the flower—to fix in his mind the exact shade, the peculiar glow, the precise intensity of scent, the beauty of curve and design in the form. His touch should assure itself of the texture and peculiarities. Next, the flower should be taken to pieces and its structure examined with the same carefulness of observation. All these should be done not as a task, but as an object of interest by skilfully arranged questions suited to the learner which will draw him on to observe and investigate one thing after the other until he has almost unconsciously mastered the whole.[5]

Not merely creative interest but also an adventure into the Gnostic or supramental manifestation of life would indicate fully well how education as Sri Aurobindo advocates for the future would be the pointer to ascent and excellence. That education is not simply eradication of ignorance but something higher and more serene would then be a challenging task for the fullness beyond. To understand the advancement of the spiritual age and appreciate it in terms of individuality where finding the true self by means of cultivation of education of the supermind would signify 'divine progression'. In Sri Aurobindo's words:

> A great access of spirituality in the past has ordinarily meant the coming of a new religion and its endeavour to impose itself upon mankind as a new universal order. This, however, was always not only a premature but a wrong crystallisation. Apart from the usual tendency of these creedal religions to turn an afterworld, their attempt is contrary to the variety of human nature and to at least one essential character of the Spirit, a spacious inner freedom and large unity into which each man must be allowed to grow according to his own nature. The one thing essential must take precedence. Therefore, the individuals who will most help the future of humanity in the new ages will be those who will recognise a spiritual evolution as the destiny and therefore the great need of the human being. That evolution or conversion—it does not greatly matter which figure we use or what theory we adopt to support it—will be their ideal and endeavour. Failures must be originally numerous in everything great and difficult, but an *a priori* declaration of impossibility is a sign of ignorance and weakness. By the doing the difficulty will be solved.

But the thing to be done is as large as human life, and therefore the individuals who lead the way will take all human life for their province. They will hold that all can be made the spirit's means of self-finding and all can be converted into its instruments of divine living. This endeavour will be a supreme and difficult labour for the individual, but much more for the race. Even for the few the ascent to the first spiritual levels would not be the end, there would be still higher levels. But once the foundation has been secured, the next develops by a progressive self-revelation, and the soul is sure of its way: the earthly evolution will have taken its great impetus upward and accomplish the revealing step in a divine progression of which the birth of thinking and aspiring man from the animal nature was only an obscure and far off promise.[6]

Indeed, education of the future cannot but be a real path-finder to progressive self-revelation. This would only lead to identification, involvement and advancement of the divine man. 'The birth of a thinking man', as Sri Aurobindo visualises as the promise and ascent ought to be the guiding spirit of the education of the future. The cycle of the society in life and education necessitates a thorough overhauling for the total inward consciousness of man. If education of the future cannot guarantee this essential end-in-view, the power of the Gnostic being would ever remain unknown and unexercised. As it is elegantly elucidated:

> To be wholly and integrally conscious of oneself and of all the truth of one's being is what is implied by the perfect emergence of the individual consciousness, and it is that towards which evolution tends. All being is one, and to be fully conscious means to be integrated with the consciousness of all, with the universal self and force and action.

The plenitude of this consciousness can only be attained by realising the identity of the individual self with the transcendent self, the supreme Reality.

This realisation demands a turning of the consciousness inward. The ordinary human consciousness is turned outward and sees the surface of things only. It recoils from entering the inner depths which appear dark and where it is afraid of losing itself. Yet the entry into this obscurity, this void, this silence is only the passage to a greater existence.

Indeed, this inward turning movement is not an imprisonment in the personal self: it is the first step towards a true universality. The law of the divine life is universality in action, organised by an all-seeing will, with the sense of the true oneness of all.

New powers of consciousness and new faculties will develop in the Gnostic being who will use them in a natural, normal and spontaneous way both for knowledge and for action.

The life of Gnostic beings might fitly be characterised as a Superhuman or divine life. But it must not be confused with past and present ideas of supermanhood.

It would be a misconception to think that a life in the full light of knowledge would lose its charm and become an insipid monotony. The Gnostic manifestation of life would be more full and fruitful and its interest more vivid than the creative interest offered to us by the world of ignorance.[7]

Education of the future as Sri Aurobindo envisions, is always a look within for a look beyond in the unending endeavour at a reconciliation between freedom and creation, exercise of the inherent law of the All Serene and Truth. It is a search beyond search for evolution of one's inner being that merges in altruism in the void beyond void.

If teachers are in a position to best facilitate the growing child in the self-discovery of excellence and ascent as Sri Aurobindo spells out as above, success in teaching becomes normal and spontaneous, transparent and poignant. If not, we have no alternative but to straightway pronounce: Teacher, teach thyself.

REFERENCES

1. "The Coming of Spiritual Age", *The Human Cycle,* Sri Aurobindo Pathamandir, Kolkata, 1972, pp. 82-83.
2. Education of the Child", *Education of the Growing Child,* Sri Aurobindo Institute of Research in Social Sciences, Sri Aurobindo Society, Pondicherry, 1996, pp. 8-9.

3. "The Coming of the Subjective Age", *The Human Cycle,* Sri Aurobindo Pathamandir, Kolkata, 1972, pp. 9-11.
4. "Education of the Child", *Education and the Growing Child,* Sri Aurobindo Institute of Research in Social Sciences, Sri Aurobindo Society, Pondicherry, 1996, pp. 3-4.
5. *Ibid.,* pp. 5-6.
6. "The Advent of the Spiritual Age", *The Human Cycle,* Sri Aurobindo Pathamandir, Kolkata, 1972, pp. 85-87.
7. Pavitra: "The Future Evolution of Man", *Education of the Future,* Sri Aurobindo Society, Pondicherry, 1996, pp. 26-27.

8
INCLUSIVE EDUCATION: PRIORITISING VIBRANT VISION

Education in the twenty-first century is yet to be meant for one and all. It is yet to appositely address the non-school going children, the drop-outs or stop-outs notwithstanding. It is yet to welcome everyone in the cathedral of learning in every nook and corner of the country. With an astounding increase in population in an already over populated country as ours is, the unheard wailings and the dormant desires of those who haplessly look forward for having a cordial and warm entry in educational institutions are yet to be sincerely negotiated. Despite the so-called sound policies of education for all under Sarva Siksha Abhiyan, one cannot but boldly assert that in practice these suffer from numerous pitfalls. As a consequence, while documents duly highlight 'total' success in adventure against illiteracy, realities glaringly present one with terribly disappointing pictures.

Admittedly, child labour and child education are showing positive symptoms of absence from schooling. Meanwhile, education for children with other constraints like physical, mental and social challenges along with other children under the same classroom or outside the classroom together is far away from living and thrilling reality. Who ignores that right from childhood the dream of a child challenged for reasons beyond her/his control is shattered in the gloom of appalling isolation and neglect in school education? Who, on the other, disagrees that, given a hearty climate of inclusive education, a Picasso or a Helen Keller in each child with learning challenges is awaiting fullness of efflorescence?

Children with special needs should, therefore, be provided with all provisions of education in an appropriate and enviable ambience of conjoint and inclusive climate of freedom and joy in learning. Not apathy, not segregation, but sympathy synchronised in endearing togetherness in and through inclusive education is the only alternative to eliminate the evils of illiteracy. It is time to create a new environment of inclusive education in every school where children with special needs receive education of the right kind and right mind to shoulder right responsibilities and perform right duties in response to right instructions and guidance programmes. In this connection, one might recall the Report to UNESCO of the International Commission on Education for the twenty-first century which significantly remarks:

> The family home is the child's first school. But, when the family environment is deficient or lacking, it is up to the school to ensure that each child's potential is realised. Special attention must be paid to all aspects of educational provision for children from disadvantaged backgrounds: street children, orphans, victims of war and other catastrophes must be the focus of concerted efforts on the part of educators. When children have special needs that cannot be diagnosed or met exclusively in the family environment, it is the responsibility of schools to provide the professional help and guidance to ensure that the talents of children with learning difficulties or physical handicaps do not go to waste.[1]

Sharing community participation and support for success in inclusive education in all schools is yet a myth almost everywhere in our country. Involvement of the immediate local community for such education further assures fulfilment of newer visions such as elimination of gender bias, firm conviction of warm access and quality effulgence besides parental education and curriculum crystallisation. As the Delors Commission characteristically suggests:

> Where education is highly valued and actively sought, the mission and goals of the school are shared and supported by the community. Thus, the increasing focus on the role of local communities needs to be encouraged and supported. Education needs to be seen by the community as applicable to their real-life situations, needs and aspirations. Specific characteristics of life in both rural and urban environments should be taken into account, through decisions about the language of instruction and a careful analysis of what needs to be adapted in the curriculum, course content, teacher training and materials. Where there is reluctance on the part of parents to send their children to school, involving the local community in the assessment of needs—through a dialogue with the authorities and other interested groups within society, and a continuation of that dialogue through use of the media, community discussions, parental education and training, and in-service teacher-training—can result in the community assuming greater responsibility for its own welfare and development.[2]

At the very crossroads of life in school education, whatever constraints in inclusive education may be there in introducing living education should be shared with an earnest zeal for bringing about a radical change in the present-day struggling scenario in Sarva Siksha Abhiyan.

The reasons why inclusive education is the only means of success in education for all irrespective of any apparent and challenging circumstances can be categorically identified as follows:

> First, education under any circumstances should never entertain biased, compartmentalised, exclusive, opportunistic and narrowness-nourished climate in any

primary seat of learning. Let the windows of inclusive education remain unbarred anywhere and everywhere.

Second, children with challenges should be encouraged to enjoy a positive learning climate in all inclusive schools. Third, care should be taken to implement latest educational strategies to serve the purpose of introducing inclusive education as a thrilling process of advancement in learning. Fourth, the educational gadgets meant for the purpose of inclusive education should be effectively reoriented and redesigned in order to serve the purpose of any learner child in the school, challenged or whatsoever.

It is time to wipe off all barriers of learning in the name of education of 'normal' children in schools exclusively meant for them. That alienation in the name of education for 'normal' children under an exclusive climate is another way of bearing the legacy of the cursed colonial system of education meant not for all but for the limited few, being itself a blatant deviation of normalcy, remains yet to be erased out from time-evasive conservative mind-sets.

A newer think-tank of illuminating and explosive education that believes in and enriches altruistic inclusive education is right now to be cultivated and skilfully disseminated. Priorities are to be directed towards making inclusive education as the only education that would christen us with a new definition of what is called normal education which always calls forth uniqueness and innovation, quality and excellence, creativity and critical thinking that outright remove all so-called handicaps in learning.

Inclusive education is now at the very juncture of ukase writ large in between public and private sector aims in educational programmes. This starts from early childhood education where specific and pinpointed suggestions can only be made through cordial debates across the table in eliminating constraints of extending a hearty welcome to introduce inclusive education. The inputs of such an endeavour can very well be forewarned with one of the latest reports on Early Childhood Education (ECE):

Broadly, it can be said that most of the private sector aims, or at least claims, to teach through the medium of English, though this is often far from the reality, while the public sector stays firmly committed to the regional language/mother tongue medium. This is often cited as the reason for the popularity of the former, since knowledge of English is seen as the main avenue to upward mobility. However, this hope is more often than not belied by the reality. Knowledge of English has thus become another major social divide, reflected in ECE as elsewhere.

Within private sector, too, there is wide variability—ranging from a handful of well-established elite schools of high quality offering excellence, to the great mass of poorly managed, overcrowded, and under-equipped 'garage' schools, which squeeze children into tiny unhygienic spaces and attempt to force-feed them with the Three R's at an unsuitably early age. A recent entry has been the 'franchised', imported, and highly expensive model catering to the new urban upper class.[3]

In the dismal scenario of education as such, what inclusive education would contribute in essence is to overhaul education where pupil segregation whatsoever is never allowed in the pretext of so-called quality control. It is time to explore a broadened quality canvas where the joy of communicated teaching-learning is vibrant with newer challenges and poignant visions of all embracing success.

Updating the curriculum in inclusive education is long overdue. For this, the first and foremost priority is a radical change in the curriculum in the present-day system of school education where children challenged physically, a mentally or in any other way are virtually left out of pursuit in education. The latest position paper of the National Focus Group on 'Systemic Reforms for Curriculum Change' distinctly admits:

Physically and mentally challenged children are effectively excluded from the schooling process due to lack of support services and inaccessibility both in terms of physical access and pedagogical strategies. Barriers to their learning and participation in the schooling process have seldom been addressed, leaving such children uncared for, and quite beyond the school.[4]

A certain pattern of overhauling the curriculum by paying attention to the five-fold strategy of bringing inclusive education in the forefront of traditional stereotyped system of education would not only benefit the desolately challenged learners but also make a bond of kinship amongst all under the fold of advancement in living and loving education:

First, priorities for educational opportunities in inclusive education should be more generously and scientifically addressed.

Second, inclusive schools should be provided with latest models of educational gadgets.

Third, care should be taken to see that freedom and joy in teaching-learning in all inclusive institutions are natural and spontaneous under a favourable climate of intimate relationship.

Fourth, textbooks for inclusive education demand radical overhauling and quality assurance. This particular matter is yet to be given its proper due.

Fifth, evaluation in inclusive education calls forth a more objective, thorough, pinpointed, experience-oriented and disciplined approach.

Teacher education for acceleration of excellence in inclusive education is yet to be seriously taken into account. At present, teachers' training institutions throughout the country do not provide teacher trainees with specialised and intensive programmes of training with a view to appropriately negotiating the needs and priorities of inclusive education. Moreover, teaching children with diverse challenges necessitates clubbing all special education institutions and/or agencies with the programmes of inclusive education so that a grand panorama of humane exercise in overcoming all barriers of ascent and excellence in education becomes a permanent reality. Due emphasis should also be given to utilisation of trained teachers in non-inclusive schools as a preliminary step to fillip welcome of inclusive education everywhere.

If education is a matter of askance and enquiry, inclusive education is definitely a more concerned matter of greater askance and enquiry in the twenty-first century because it opens a newer window of access to children with special needs. Societal awareness and community participation in such a conjoint endeavour would also ensure undertaking a more positive role in making education for all an all-embracing success.

The aesthetics of inclusive education is yet to be cultivated with due respect and sincerity. Unless an enlightened approach to beauty and goodness side by side with adherence to the great truth of we-ness is adorned in the principles and practice of inclusive education, there is every possibility of shaking hands as it were with drabness and monotony, indifference and passivity. Meanwhile, many a child flower with promises to bloom in all brightness would wail: "O dark, dark, dark!"

It is time to realise the present-day reality in the state of affairs in inclusive education. It is a simple truth that inclusive education is yet to become inclusive in our educational institutions. The mindsets of many a person even associated with educational plans and programmes of action for total education necessitates a reshuffling of vision for inclusive education which is not for the time being and should never be considered a patchwork in education for all. Let the individual priorities in education in case of every child be given appropriate emphasis so that learning becomes a matter of everlasting interest and joy. From this viewpoint on the reality that we normally consider very essential, it has been rightly observed:

> The reality is that most education services in the world are not inclusive. Instead, they follow traditional

methods of teaching and organisation, leaving behind many learners—those who are excluded from mainstream school entirely, and those who are enrolled in or attend school but are excluded from learning for lack of a responsible, child-centred pedagogy. Separate education programmes are sometimes available for children living on the street, for working children or for children with disabilities, but often, especially in poorer countries with limited education funds, these children are neglected. IE[Inclusive Education] also acknowledges that forcing children to attend segregated special schools, may violate their rights to community involvement, and that this separation tends to reinforce societal prejudice against children who are *different* due to poverty, social background or disabilities. IE accepts that 80 per cent of all children with disabilities can study in mainstream schools with a minimum of *transformation* to the schools or to the education programme—and that the actual barrier to their education is not one of disability, but of failure in methodology and organisation of the education services. Changing methodology and organisation into a more flexible and child-friendly one not only benefits previously excluded children, but is beneficial for all children. Schools reflect the diversity in society and as such they should be able to address diversity in an inclusive way. Some children are very clever, others may have extraordinary creative skill, some children speak in a different mother-tongue, while others move with their families from one place to another—each of these children has individual learning needs that all mainstream schools should be able to address adequately.

It may also be helpful to mention that IE is not *participation* in another term often used in development and education circles, and should not be considered interchangeable with inclusion. While the former seeks to ensure that learning and development are not top down, but are rather shaped by the ideas, feedback and initiative of those who are the most marginalised, and to ensure that the system is flexible enough to optimise participation for everyone.

Thus, inclusive education is an approach to improve the education system by limiting and removing barriers to learning and acknowledging individual children's needs and potential. The goal of this approach is to make a significant impact on the educational opportunities of those (1) who attend school but who, for different reasons, do not achieve adequately, and those (2) who are not attending school, but who could attend if families, communities, schools and education systems were more responsive to their requirements.[5]

For newer values in inclusive education, we cannot but explore newer visions and possibilities, newer guidelines and more poignant promises yet to be identified in terms of changing realities in the twenty-first century. A pre-awareness to the following in piloting any project on inclusive education as suggested below might pave a sound foundation and prospect in diverse frontiers of development in education:

1. *Relying on awareness raising to inspire teachers to take on IE approaches on a goodwill basis.* Teachers have a right to quality teacher training and need to be trained on how to teach in an inclusive way. They must also be offered practical, continued support in their efforts.
2. *Ignoring the importance of community Early Child Development (ECD) activities and preschools.* This may be seen as a 'luxury' when the government is already concerned about its commitment to ensure universal primary education. Nevertheless, ECD and preschool activities can provide vital early intervention, especially in facilitating positive changes in the attitudes and perceptions of teachers, parents and children to view diversity in terms of different socio-economic backgrounds, ethnic or religious background, gender and (dis)abilities etc., as an enrichment instead of a problem.

3. *Assuming that the main IE focus should be on children with disabilities, rather than on the learning of all children in the classroom.* When teaching focuses mainly on the needs of disadvantaged children, too much of the teacher's attention will be taken away from the other children. The aim is not to give the child with special needs a better deal than others, but to give it the same chances as others and while raising the standard of education of all children.
4. *Assuming that there is bound to be strong lasting prejudice,* naturally, families will be against a programme where the inclusion of children with problems means that their children's overall education becomes of a lower standard. However, when IE results in an improved school where good teachers teach effectively for all children, failure rates as well as prejudice will decline. Conversely, prejudice and misconceptions must not be overlooked, and efforts to combat these must take into account the way in which they are culturally manifested.
5. *Assuming that other children do not face similar difficulties as children with disabilities,* the number of children who fail in school becomes high. IE is also about reducing general failure and drop out rates for all students. Techniques that schools can use to help children with learning problems and disabilities are responsive teaching-learning approaches that are just as useful for other children, and will ultimately reduce the failure rate.[6]

Admittedly, inclusive education should have a vision that advances beyond the present with all promises vibrantly fulfilled. It is not simply a challenge but an eventuality that the march for advancement in education is holistically shared and conjoined in a very disciplined and crystallised manner. Conversely, if inclusive education is caged and cornered and thus allowed to suffer from sub-standard, parochial and camouflaged endeavour, the very term 'inclusive' loses its qualitative ends-in-view.

Do we whole-heartedly feel and seriously ponder?

REFERENCES

1. *Learning: The Treasure Within*, UNESCO, 1996, p. 122.
2. *Ibid.*, pp. 122-23.
3. *National Curriculum Framework 2005*, Position Paper, "National Focus Group on Early Childhood Education", National Council of Educational Research and Training, New Delhi, 2006, p. 15.)
4. National Focus Group, *National Curriculum Framework 2005*, NCERT, New Delhi, 2006, p. 4.
5. Sanat Kumar Ghosh: "Inclusive Education: A Conceptual Framework", *Inclusive Education: The Indian Context*, Progressive Publishers, Kolkata, 2003, pp. 8-9.
6. *Ibid.*, pp. 71-72.

9

LIVING EDUCATION: VIVEKANANDA'S VIEWPOINTS

Education is a quest for advancement. To Swami Vivekananda, it is a quest for efflorescence and perfection. Mere knowledge for the sake of knowledge is no education of living resonance. For education to be living and pulsating, it must respond to the Infinite Self which is 'the vital force'—the Prana.

True education, as Vivekananda advocates, is the most effective means of grasping the truth of One Absolute Existence, and, for this end-in-view, grasping the Prana wherein the forces of the universe diverse and different exist. In analysing the infinite ocean of the Prana as the most prized goal of education for manifestation of perfection, he characteristically observes:

> The Prana is the vital force in every being. Thought is the finest and highest action of Prana. Thought, again, as we see, is not all. There is also what we call instinct or unconscious thought, the lowest plane of action. If a mosquito stings us, our hand will strike it automatically, instinctively. This is one expression of thought. All reflex actions of the body belong to this plane of thought. There is again the other plane of thought, the conscious. I reason, I judge, I think, I see the pros and cons of certain things, yet that is not all. We know that reason is limited. Reason can go only to a certain extent, beyond that it cannot reach. The circle within which it runs is very very limited indeed. Yet

at the same time, we find facts rush into this circle. Like the coming of comets certain things come into this circle; it is certain they come from outside the limit, although our reason cannot go beyond. The causes of the phenomena intruding themselves in this small limit are outside this limit. The mind can exist on a still higher plane, the superconscious. When the mind has attained to that state, which is called Samadhi—perfect concentration, superconsciousness—it goes beyond the limits of reason, and comes face to face with facts which no instinct or reason can ever know. All manipulations of the subtle forces of the body, the different manifestations of Prana, if trained, give a push to the mind, help it to go up higher, and become superconscious, from where it acts.[1]

The quest for the ideal in education, the very living entity, is the mind. It is not mere knowing the mind where the purpose of education is over. It is, on the other hand, the beginning from where the quest for the infinite power in every living being starts. No competition, no utilitarian approach as education in the modern era strongly approves and aimlessly promulgates, but education for regulating the mind to be prepared for the unending quest for super-consciousness is what the living education of Vivekananda always upholds.

Admittedly, Vivekananda directs our wholehearted attention to the fact that it is the essential end-in-view of education to empower everyone to realise the infinite power of the mind. It perfects our inner and outer instruments contributing to the perfection of the oceanic mind. As he adroitly elucidates:

> All knowledge is within [the] mind. Who saw knowledge in the stone, or astronomy in the star? It is all in the human being.

Let us realise [that] we are the infinite power. Who put a limit to the power of mind? Let us realise we are all mind. Every drop has the whole of the ocean in it. That is the mind of man. The Indian mind reflects upon these [powers and potentialities] and wants to bring [them] all out. For himself he does not care what happens. It will take a great length of time [to reach perfection]. If it takes fifty thousand years, what of that! .....

The very foundation of society, the formation of it, makes the defect. [Perfection] is only possible if the mind of man is changed, if he, of his own sweet will, changes his mind; and the great difficulty is, neither can he force his own mind.

* * * *   * * * *

Education is not filling the mind with a lot of facts. Perfecting the instrument and getting complete mastery of my own mind [is the ideal of education]. If I want to concentrate my mind upon a point, it goes there, and the moment I call, it is free [again]. ....

That is the great difficulty. By great struggle we get a certain power of concentration, the power of attachment of the mind to certain things. But then there is not the power of detachment. I would give half my life to take my mind off that object! I cannot. It is the power of concentration and attachment as well as the power of detachment [that we must develop]. [If] the man [is] equally powerful in both—that man has attained manhood. You cannot make him miserable even if the whole universe tumbles about his ears. What books can teach you that? You may read any amount of books. ...Crowd into the child fifty thousand words a moment, teach him all the theories and philosophies. ... There is only one science that will teach him facts, and that is psychology. ... And the work begins with control of the breath.

Slowly and gradually you get into the chambers of the mind and gradually get control of the mind. It is a long, [hard struggle]. It must not be taken up as something curious.[2]

Living education, as Vivekananda observes, is an eternal quest for Truth. It is to drive away what appears to be Truth and is never so because it fails to drive away sentimentalism that is happy with crudity and meaninglessness. Education must pave the avenues of eliminating mere visions and effulging Truth that stands for 'Eternal Love and Service Free' as he clearly spells out:

> Awake, arise, and dream no more!
> This is the land of dreams, where Karma
> Weaves unthreaded garlands with our thoughts
> Of flowers sweet or noxious, and none
> Has root or stem, being born in naught, which
> The softest breath of Truth drives back to
> Primal nothingness. Be bold, and face
> The Truth! Be one with it! Let visions cease,
> Or, if you cannot, dream but truer dreams,
> Which are Eternal Love and Service Free.[3]

The education that India needs in the new millennium is that which makes everyone sincere and responsive to living reality where the inherent components of perfection beckon for efflorescence and fullness. Spread of education presupposes spread of genuine involvement of one and all in the quest for altruism.

Vivekananda's own concern for vibrant education is based on reality that shows how the invaluable spirit of reverence as has been cultivated in our country from time immemorial necessitates a strong and positive revival and research. Analysing the positive outcome of education of understanding and appreciating the spirit of Brahman in everyone of us and that of reverence as we badly need today, he significantly points out:

> Travelling through many cities of Europe and observing in them the comforts and education of even the poor people, there was brought to my mind the state of our own poor people, and I used to shed tears. What made the difference/education was the answer I got. Through education comes faith in one's own Self, and through faith in one's own Self the inherent Brahman is waking up in them, while the Brahman in us is gradually becoming dormant. In New York I used to

> observe the Irish colonists come—downtrodden, haggard-looking, destitute of all possessions at home, penniless, and wooden-headed—with their only belongings, a stick and a bundle of rags hanging at the end of it, fright in their steps, alarm in their eyes. A different spectacle in six months—the man walks upright, his attire is changed! In his eyes and steps there is no more sign of fright. What is the cause? Our Vedanta says that that Irishman was kept surrounded by contempt in his own country—the whole of nature was telling him with one voice, "Pat, you have no more hope, you are born a slave and will remain so." Having been thus told from his birth, Pat believed in it and hypnotised himself that he was very low, and the Brahman in him shrank away. While no sooner had he landed in America than he heard the shout going up on all sides, "Pat, you are a man as we are. It is man who has done all, a man like you and me can do everything: have courage!" pat raised his head and saw that it was so, the Brahman within woke up. Nature herself spoke, as it were, "Arise, awake, and stop not till the goal is reached" (Katha Upanishad, I. ii. 4.)

Likewise, the education that our boys receive is very negative. The schoolboy learns nothing, but has everything of his own broken down—want of Shraddha is the result.[4]

For living education as Vivekananda affirms in the context of eliminating negative education, the importance of exercise in creativity that cares for freedom of thought and expression can hardly be denied. In fact, the religion of education indicates how artificialities are replaced by originalities in diverse directions with appropriate handling of individual intellect. As he significantly asserts:

> We have to do only so much for the boys that they may learn to apply their own intellect to the proper use of their hands, legs, ears, eyes, etc., and finally everything will become easy. But the root is religion. Religion is as the rice, and everything else, like the

> curries. Taking only curries causes indigestion, and so is the case of taking rice alone. Our pedagogues are making parrots of our boys and ruining their brains by cramming a lot of subjects into them. Looking from one standpoint, you should rather be grateful to the Viceroy for his proposal of reforming the University system, which means practically abolishing higher education; the country will, at least, feel some relief by having breathing time. Goodness gracious! What a fuss and fury about graduating, and after a few days, all cools down! And after all that, what is it they learn but that what religion and customs we have are all bad, and what the Westerners have are all good! At last they cannot keep the wolf from the door! What does this matter if this higher education remains or goes? It would be better if the people got a little technical education, so that they might find work and earn their bread instead of dawdling about and crying for service.[5]

Vibrant education—living, pulsating and thrilling— cannot but respond to understanding the Self which, according to Vivekananda, is the All Powerful which is always within every-one of us. The education that teaches us to be beyond work in order to reach the pinnacle of non-attachment shows the way of this understanding. That is living education. That is education par excellence. That is to explore 'the gymnasium of the world'. Vivekananda asserts on that education which accelerates our little self to be in an endless quest for the Supreme Self, 'the ever active Providence':

> The highest men cannot work, for in them there is no attachment. Those whose soul is gone into the Self, those whose desires are confined in the Self, who have become ever associated with the Self, for them there is no work. In so working we should never think that we can help on even the last thing in this universe. We cannot. We only help ourselves in this gymnasium of the world. This is the proper attitude of work. If we work in this way, if we always remember that our

> present opportunity to work thus is a privilege which has been given to us, we shall never be attached to anything. Millions like you and me think that we are great people in the world; but we all die and in five minutes the world forgets us. But the life of God is infinite. "Who can live a moment, breathe a moment, if this all powerful One does not will it?" He is the ever active Providence. All power is His and within His command. Through His command the windows blow, the sun shines, the earth lives, and death stalks upon earth. He is the all in all; He is all and in all. We can only worship Him. Give up all fruits of work; do good for its own sake; then alone will come perfect non-attachment. The bonds of the heart will thus break, and we will reap perfect freedom.[6]

The quest for living education is, indeed, the tireless endeavour at fulfilment of the aesthetic vision through the scanner of good and evil in terms of the teaching of the Vedanta philosophy of excellence and ascent. Vivekananda identifies it as the 'living blessing' which shows the way of self-crystallisation by means education that cares for the good by eliminating the evil. As he characteristically elucidates:

> It is a lie to say that I am a man or a woman, or to say that I belong to this country or that. All the world is my country, the whole universe is mine, because I have clothed myself with it as my body. Yet we see that there are people in this world who are ready to assert these doctrines, and at the same time do things which we should call filthy; and if we ask them why they do so, they tell us that it is our delusion and that they can do nothing wrong. What is the test by which they are to be judged? The test is here.

Though good and evil are both conditioned manifestations of the soul, yet evil is the most external coating, and good is the nearer coating of the real man, the Self. And unless a man cuts through the layer of evil he cannot reach the layer of good, and unless he has passed through both the layers of good and evil he cannot reach the Self. He who reaches the Self, what remains attached to him? A little Karma, a little bit of the momentum of past life, but it is all good momentum. Until the bad momentum is entirely worked out and past impurities are entirely burnt, it is impossible for any man to see or realise truth. So, what is left attached to the man who has reached the Self and seen the truth is the remnant of the good impressions of past life, the good momentum. Even if he lives in the body and works incessantly, he works only to do good; his lips speak only benediction to all; his hands do only good works; his mind can only think good thoughts; his presence is a blessing wherever he goes. He is himself a living blessing. Such a man will, by his very presence, change even the most wicked persons into saints. Even if he does not speak, his very presence will be a blessing to mankind. Can such a man do any evil; can they do wicked deeds? There is, you must remember, all the difference of pole to pole between realisation and mere talking. Any fool can talk. Even parrots talk. Talking is one thing, and realising is another. Philosophies, and doctrines, and arguments, and books, and theories, and churches, and sects, and all these things are good in their own way; but when that realisation comes, these things drop away. For instance, maps are good, but when you see the country itself, and look again at the maps, what a great difference you find! So those that have realised truth do not require the ratiocinations of logic and all other gymnastics of the intellect to make them understand the truth; it is to them the life of their lives, concretised, made more than tangible.[7]

Prioritising the heart instead of the head so that the education of the heart becomes the education of humanism in the true sense of the term is one of the most significant points of Vivekananda's philosophy of vibrant education. His concern for education as it is well-known is man making and character building. Unless education is in perfect tune with the heart that cares and ennobles the inherent greatness, the very divinity of man, it is absolutely meaningless. This is why the end-in-view of all efforts at vibrant education should always be how to glorify education of the heart in reality. In the incomparable and poignant words of Vivekananda:

When there is conflict between the heart and the brain, let the heart be followed, because intellect has only one state, reason, and within that, intellect works, and cannot get beyond. It is the heart that takes one to the highest plane, which intellect an never reach; it goes beyond intellect, and reaches to what is called inspiration. Intellect can never become inspired; only the heart where it is enlightened, becomes inspired. An intellectual, heartless man never becomes an inspired man. It is always the heart that speaks in the man of love; it discovers a greater instrument than intellect can give you, the instrument of inspiration. Just as intellect is the instrument of knowledge, so is the heart the instrument of inspiration. In a lower state it is a much weaker instrument than intellect. An ignorant man knows nothing, but he is a little emotional by nature. Compare him with a great professor—what wonderful power the latter possesses! But the professor is bound by his intellect, and he can be a devil and an intellectual man at the same time; but the man of heart can never be a devil; no man with emotion was ever a devil. Properly cultivated, the heart can be changed, and will go beyond intellect; it will be changed into inspiration. Man will have to go beyond intellect in the end. The knowledge of man, his powers of perception, of reasoning and intellect and heart, all are busy churning the milk of the world. Out of long churning comes butter, and this butter is God. Men of heart get the "butter", and the "buttermilk" is left for the intellectual.[8]

That true and living education is essentially 'a plunge into the unknown and unknowable' is what Vivekananda categorically asserts. If it is not a limitless search for the unknown it loses its very purpose of how it leads to light. Little by little this quest for the unknown must be guaranteed and consolidated. Little by little this endeavour should be a part and parcel of life. Little by little it should be the be all and end all of life. Then it genuinely leads to understanding the religion of education which is the religion of appreciating the vision of the 'super-sensuous' as Vivekananda explicitly spells out:

> This adventure of ours, the universe of the senses, the rational, the intellectual, is bound on both sides by the illimitable, the unknowable, the ever unknown. Herein is the search, herein are the enquiries, here are the facts; from this comes the light which is known to the world as religion. Essentially, however, religion belongs to the super-sensuous and not to the sense plane. It is beyond all reasoning, and not on the plane of intellect. It is a vision, an inspiration, a plunge into the unknown and unknowable, making the unknowable more than known, for it can never be "known". This search has been in the human mind, as I believe, from the very beginning of humanity. There cannot have been human reasoning and intellect in any period of the world's history without this struggle, this search beyond. In our little universe, this human mind, we see a thought arise. Whence, it rises we do not know, and when it disappears, where it goes, we know not either. The macrocosm and the microcosm are, as it were, in the same groove, passing through the same stages, vibrating in the same key.[9]

Education to be rightly steered towards the enviable new directions ought to be the education of the beyond. What has been expressed, explored, cultivated and appreciated in and through education is not enough. In fact, it is the beginning of our journey. The beckoning of the beyond, the unexpressed and the undiscovered cannot, under any circumstances, be ignored and averted for it shows the path of transfer and transcendence from the material world of ours to the Absolute or Unknowable, Infinite or All Serene. Vivekananda's own elucidation on this point is remarkable:

> This present, this expressed, is one part of that unexpressed. The sense universe is, as it were, only

> one portion, one bit of that infinite spiritual universe projected into the plane of sense consciousness. How can this little bit of projection can be explained, be understood without knowing that which is beyond? It is said of Socrates that one-day while lecturing at Athens, he met a Brahmana who had travelled into Greece, and Socrates told the Brahmana that the greatest study of mankind is man. And the Brahmana sharply retorted, "How can you know man until you know God?" This God, this eternally Unknowable, or Absolute, or Infinite, or without name—you may call Him by what name you like—is the rationale, the only explanation, the raison d'etre of that which is known and knowable, this present life. Take anything before you, the most material thing—take one of these most materialistic sciences, such as chemistry or physics, astronomy or biology—study it, push the study forward and forward, and the gross forms will begin to melt and become finer and finer, until they come to a point where you are bound to make a tremendous leap from the material things to the immaterial. The gross melts into the fine, physics into metaphysics, in every department of knowledge.[10]

For a new education of the new millennium with the promise of perfection with living resonance, Vivekananda wants it to be truly christened with transfer and transcendence. It must cater to social awareness. The world is looking forward to a new education where the millions of the world come under the one conjoint and communicated global-friendly world of cordiality and pursuit for ascent and excellence limitless and adventurous.

Indeed, Vivekananda shows us the ever dynamic avenue of excellence beyond excellence in and through living and altruistic education in we-having, we-loving and we-feeling. As he significantly upholds:

> The education which does not help the common mass of people to equip themselves for the struggle for life,

which does not bring the strength of character, a spirit of philanthropy, and the courage of a lion—is it worth the name? Real education is that which enables one to stand on one's own legs. The education that you are receiving now in schools and colleges is only making you a race of dyspeptics. You are working like machines merely, and living a jelly-fish existence.

The peasant, the shoe-maker, the sweeper, and such other lower classes in India have much greater capacity for work and self-reliance than you. They have been silently working through long ages and producing the entire wealth of the land, without a word of complaint. Very soon they will get above you in position. Gradually capital is drifting into their hands, and they are not so much troubled with wants as you are. Modern education has changed your fashion, but new avenues of wealth lie yet undiscovered for want of the inventive genius. You have so long oppressed these forbearing masses; now is the time for their retribution. And you will become extinct in your vain search for employment, making it the be-all and end-all of your life.[11]

When would we very sincerely strive for living education?

REFERENCES

1. Swami Vivekananda: The Complete Works of Swami Vivekananda, Advaita Ashrama. Calcutta, *Mayavati Memorial Edition*, 1989, Vol. I, p. 150.
2. *Ibid.*, pp. 509-11.
3. "To the Awakened India", *Ibid.*, Vol. IV, pp. 388-89.
4. *Ibid.*, pp. 483-484.
5. *Ibid.*, Vol. V, pp. 366-67.
6. *Ibid.*, Vol. I, pp. 106-07.
7. *Ibid.*, Vol. II, pp. 283-84.
8. *Ibid.*, Vol. I, pp. 412-13.
9. *Ibid.*, Vol. IV, p. 203.
10. *Ibid.*, p. 204.
11. *Ibid.*, Vol. VII, pp. 147-48.

10
RELEVANCE OF TAGORE'S CREATIVE THINKING IN THE NEW MILLENNIUM

Unlike any other educational thinker and philosopher, Rabindranath Tagore, himself an unparalleled educational map as it were in the world of education for creative and critical thinking, is yet to be studied with serenity and poignancy from national and global excellence and ascent in education in particular. His thoughts and experiments in education are quite distinct from the usual patterns and courses of education as we still now encounter and experience at least from the point of view that education should never be passive but active, not mechanical but thrilling and pulsating, not dead but living, not dry but vigorous and fresh, not forced but spontaneous, and, over and above, not imitative but unendingly creative and critical.

That creative thinking ceaselessly contributes to the making and remaking of man is the forte in Tagore's ends-in-view in education. He earnestly prays for the only aspiring unison between life and education which are poles apart in our bankruptcies in education. Nearly eighty years ago, exactly in 1929, he wanted to draw our attention to this prayer in his pioneering essay *Sikshar Herpher* ("Vicissitudes of Education"). Creative to the end or better to say to the end beyond end, his versatility like his life, marvels and tensions are the prized dividends not for him alone but for the whole of humanity.

Education for the child, as Tagore thought and experimented cannot but be entirely creative. It is not a mere theory or a philosophical ideology. To him, it is a lesson to be learnt out of one's own, very own, inherent response in the efflorescence of a flower or in the writing of a poem as the sub-conscious mind is like a blackbird's bill always seeking the enviable prize for perfect self-expression. Like a 'torn out line of a verse', the wailings of the absence of creative thinking in worthwhile manifestation always haunted him. The so-called schools with caged and walled prison-houses from ten to five – *dasta panchtar Andaman* or *harinbarir prachir* – as he had appropriately identified hardly care for emancipation of creative thinking, the essence of education.

For education of sympathy which is the heart of education, Tagore advocated for creativity from seven-fold point of view:

First, education should always be in symphony with Nature. There is no other teacher greater than Nature. In Tagore's words, "We must be natural with Nature and human with human sensibilities." Indeed, born as we are in the midst of Nature, it is essential that all education must be in close communion with her for she never betrays the heart that loves her. Therefore, the education that we receive under the open sky in the vast panorama of the moon and the stars, the sun and the trees, the plants and the flowers, in the twittering of birds or in the stillness at noon is a serene lesson of inwardness rich with the promise of the efflorescence of the creative mind bereft of which the soul of education cannot be the education of the soul.

Second, as education is consciousness of the self well-supported by self-identity, self-study, self-help, self-activity and self-development and never a parasitical tool for transitory success or happiness, it must prepare one for an unending adventure within. It must act like a touchstone for whatever brings forth stick-to-itiveness to discipline and diligence, purity and cadence, and continual crystallisation of the self by means of exercise of best thoughts, best vision, best emotions and best sensibilities. If our education and creative thinking fall short of undertaking and fulfilling the objectives as above, it loses the very spirit of its connotation – growth and development.

Third, education for the sake of education as a matter of fact is alien to Tagore's philosophy of education as it is rest assured with 'the parrot's training', having something like a finished product, workaholic happiness, yielding to hydraulic pressure under streamlined and career-conscious mechanical endeavour, thanks, of course, to an era of super-computer consciousness! When would the creative mind be saved from *parasonar jantakal* – the death-trap of erudition and edification of man?

Fourth, education cannot but be the essence of fullness of personality, and, for this end-in-view, it must enable one to exercise creative and critical thinking. The finer components of creative and aesthetic thinking like truth, goodness, beauty, modesty, empathy, magnanimity and so on which also stand for moral values and defy all definitions await nursling with the education of togetherness where creative thinking is always a wonderful conjoint, communicated and living experience. Tagore always reminds us: "Apathy and ignorance are the worst forms of bondage for man." How can we really educate ourselves unless we become champions of creative togetherness in life and work, contemplation and dedication to the living spirit of education?

Fifth, with education that fosters creative thinking, the emancipation of the little 'I' for the manifestation of the greater 'We' not only serves as an objective but also as a sacred mission for fulfilment. One wonders how, despite all constraints, Tagore submitted his proposal for non-formal education of the hapless *hoi polloi* in 1933 to the – then Education Minister of undivided Bengal and involved great scholars of different disciplines because he wanted that the spirit of creative thinking of the deprived must be honoured and stimulated as a positive process of dissemination of education through *Lokasiksha-Sansad* (The Council of People's Education). Who cares for such an adventure of education for development of creative thinking for all as was envisioned and translated into incomparable reality by the Poet of the Earth (*Prithivir Kavi*)?

Sixth, education is an inward force eternal, vigorous, enlightened and poignant. For such a force, cultivation of creative thinking and critical appreciation is more than compulsory as it pronounces the psychological truth that everyone is blessed with uniqueness. This unique entity is identified in the Upanishad as energy—*praiti*—unmatched, self-defining, undying, natural and spontaneous. Unless education is justified with creativity and critical consciousness, *praiti* suffers, commonality stealthily creeps in and, as an unavoidable consequence, education for freshness and inquisitiveness, vigour and inwardness, serenity and righteousness turn-out to be a myth. An outright iconoclast, Tagore has time and again protested against meaningless and lifeless education that never cares for the 'banished soul' as he has appositely identified, hopelessly pining for the appalling absence of creative thinking. When would everyone of us respond to Tagore's clarion call of ceaseless striving for being an *atmavit* in the perfection of creative thinking?

Seventh, if education is a process of one's very own, then there is no room for artificiality—a fact to which Tagore has time and again wanted to draw our attention. This is why he has always advocated for ingenuity in education by means of careful and continuous exercise of creative thinking in an atmosphere of absolute freedom and joy. Let the child enjoy the warmth of living and living Nature in its natural and spontaneous efflorescence of creative thinking. Let its teacher, too, be a significant and sensitive partner to creativity, whose childlike simplicity—*chhelemanushi*—creditably eliminates the identity of being a pre-historic animal—*pragaitihasik prani* as he has referred to in *Ashramer Siksha* ("The Education of the Ashrama"). That an inner discipline ardent, harmonious, and, of course, well-nourished in the vibrant spirit of creative consciousness is the most successful means of education for fullness remains to be wholeheartedly accepted and translated into reality in our utilitarian craziness and production-prone temperamental drabness. When would we look back in askance and look anew and afresh in advancement of education for creative marvels?

Admittedly, we are at the crossroads of education for creative thinking in the new millennium, when education for self-realisation in and through education for that of soul-consciousness enriched with realisation of love, beauty and the Infinite becomes an ever abiding reality. At the same time, the vision of the society crystallised in the inner vision of creative consciousness for which education has much more to contribute awaits the new millennium to be buoyant with the spirit of freedom and joy awaiting effulgence in all spontaneity and serenity. Freedom in thought and expression, in creativity and critical thinking is as Tagore has always emphasised the very positive symptom of living and thrilling education. There is no denying the fact that the new millennium is yet to rise up to eliminate lifeless, mechanical and passive education that practically pays no dividend except joyless and utilitarian affluence.

Transfer and transcendence in education through poignancy and transparency as Tagore always welcomes for fullness in creative thinking as its essentials and guiding principles cannot but be nurtured now and for ever. He substantiates the proposition by incorporating joy as the latter through creativity makes one fearless in exploring the self for the All Serene. He also draws our attention to the endless power of joy in creativity by referring to the Upanishad: *Anandang Brahmano vidvan na vibheti kutaschana.*

The quest for the Infinite to encounter the man of the heart expanding and enriching *chidakas,* the firmament of the mind, is one of the fundamental ends-in-view of creative thinking for which Tagore ever remains an unparalleled exponent. If education fails to do justice to it, what is education for the new millennium?

Index